*Lives of Notable
Asian Americans*

The Asian American Experience

Spacious Dreams
 The First Wave of Asian Immigration

Journey to Gold Mountain
 The Chinese in 19th-Century America

Raising Cane
 The World of Plantation Hawaii

Issei and Nisei
 The Settling of Japanese America

From the Land of Morning Calm
 The Koreans in America

Ethnic Islands
 The Emergence of Urban Chinese America

In the Heart of Filipino America
 Immigrants from the Pacific Isles

India in the West
 South Asians in America

Democracy and Race
 Asian Americans and World War II

Strangers at the Gates Again
 Asian American Immigration After 1965

From Exiles to Immigrants
 The Refugees from Southeast Asia

Breaking Silences
 Asian Americans Today

Lives of Notable Asian Americans
 Arts/Entertainment/Sports

Lives of Notable Asian Americans
 Business/Science/Politics

Lives of Notable Asian Americans
 Literature and Education

Lives of Notable
Asian Americans

LITERATURE AND EDUCATION

Christina Chiu

EDITORIAL CONSULTANT: RONALD TAKAKI
PROFESSOR OF ETHNIC STUDIES
AT THE UNIVERSITY OF CALIFORNIA, BERKELEY

Chelsea House Publishers

New York ✳ Philadelphia

On the cover Amy Tan, Maxine Hong Kingston, Dwight Okita.

Chelsea House Publishers

EDITORIAL DIRECTOR   Richard Rennert
EXECUTIVE MANAGING EDITOR   Karyn Gullen Browne
COPY CHIEF   Robin James
PICTURE EDITOR   Adrian G. Allen
CREATIVE DIRECTOR   Robert Mitchell
ART DIRECTOR   Joan Ferrigno
PRODUCTION MANAGER   Sallye Scott

The Asian American Experience

SENIOR EDITOR   Jake Goldberg
SERIES DESIGN   Marjorie Zaum

Staff for *Lives Of Notable Asian Americans:
Literature And Education*
EDITORIAL ASSISTANT   Scott D. Briggs
PICTURE RESEARCHER   ·Pat Burns

3   5   7   9   8   6   4   2

Library of Congress Cataloging-in-Publication Data
Chiu, Christina.
  Lives of notable Asian Americans: literature and education/
Christina Chiu.
    p. cm. — (The Asian American experience)
  Includes bibliographical references and index.
Summary: Discusses the lives of some Asian Americans primarily
known for their writing, including Amy Tan, David Henry Hwang,
Bharati Mukherjee, Jessica Hagedorn, and Laurence Yep.
ISBN 0-7910-2182-3.
   I. American literature—Asian American authors—History and
criticism—Juvenile literature. 2. Asian Americans—Intellectual life—
Juvenile literature. 3. Asian Americans in literature—Juvenile literature.
4. Asian Americans—Education—Juvenile literature. [I. Asian
Americans—Biography. 2. Authors, American.] I. Title.
II. Series: Asian American experience (New York, N.Y.)
PS508.A8C48 1995   94-45842
810.9'895—dc20   CIP
                                                        AC

Contents

Best-selling author Amy Tan is photographed in Dallas, Texas, on a promotional tour for the movie The Joy Luck Club.

*Amy
Tan*

"FROM THE TIME I WAS SIX," AMY TAN HAS SAID, "I WAS led to believe that I would grow up a neurosurgeon by trade and a concert pianist by hobby." Success, in the opinion of her parents, meant to become a doctor. There was no other way. Only then would they think that their daughter would be financially stable enough to take care of herself, and later, her retired parents. How is it, then, that Amy Tan went on to become one of the country's best-selling authors? "The question is," Amy says, "what in our lives is fate, the circumstances we're born into, and what are the things that we have really chosen at those important turns in our lives?"

Her two novels, *The Joy Luck Club* and *The Kitchen God's Wife*, reveal the universal bonds and conflicts of mother-daughter relationships. In these books, Tan explored the pain and struggles between mother and daughter, but also the evolution of a bonding relationship between two women. In fact, Tan wrote *The Kitchen God's Wife* with the intent of documenting her mother's life story. In so doing, Tan made the "turn" to writing as she redefined—for her mother as well as for herself—the meaning of success.

Amy Tan was born in Oakland, California, in 1952. Her father, John Tan, worked in China for the United States Information Service before World War II. He then immigrated to America in 1947, where he became an engineer and served as a Baptist minister. Tan's mother came to the United States in 1942 shortly before Mao Zedong and the Communist party seized control of China. Here Tan's mother, Daisy, met John Tan and they married. They started a new life together and had three children in the States, but Daisy's three daughters from a previous marriage would remain incessantly in her memories. At night, she would dream of the three daughters that she was forced to leave behind.

Tan would not find out about her mother's secret until she was 14. Her father and her 16-year-old brother, Peter, developed brain cancer, and her father's death followed her brother's by about six months. It was after the loss of her husband that Mrs. Tan finally told her children about their half-sisters. "My mother's version of it," Tan has said in an interview, "is that one day she told my brother and me the news and asked if we had any questions. And I said: 'No. Can I go out and play?' My version is that my mother and I were having a horrible argument, and she said: 'I wish I'd never come to this country. I have other daughters who would have been obedient daughters.' " It was through her mother's announcement that Tan learned of her mother's first husband, his abusive conduct, and the divorce that, according to Chinese law at the time, forced her to give up custody of the children to their father.

The news stunned Tan at the time. Who were these "obedient" daughters who were so good? Growing up trying to be "American," had meant "choosing the American things—hot dogs and apple pie—and ignoring the Chinese offerings." She responded only to her American name, Amy, ignoring her Chinese name, An Mei, which means "blessing from America." Much of this self-hate, she recalls now, came about after she moved into white neighborhoods, where she was at times called "Chink." If she stopped eating a certain amount of Chinese food, Tan had wondered, would the Chineseness go away? In her teens, when people started to date, she started to ask herself if the reason she never got asked on a date was because she was Chinese, or whether it was because she "was the nerd who raised her hand in class."

Tan had even blamed her mother for all the troubles she was having, because her mother was "so Chinese" while Tan regarded herself as totally American. Tensions rose between Tan and her mother. The sudden news that there were other children affected Tan strongly. The other daughters made Tan feel like she was the "wicked" daughter; the one her mother got stuck with. Tan then tried to be the "obedient" girl that her mother wanted her to be.

After the deaths of her son and husband, Daisy Tan called in geomancers, people who study the position of your house and the things in it in relation to the wind, water, and the surrounding natural environment. Daisy Tan wanted to see if there was anything wrong with the "qi," or energy, in their home and turned to this ancient Chinese belief system for help and protection. "Here she was," Tan describes her mother, "the wife of a Baptist minister trying to follow all the proper Christian ways, now bringing out all the superstitious ways that had been there all along." Daisy's reborn faith in her traditional beliefs led her to move, taking 15-year-old Amy and her younger brother to live in Europe. "She told me this theory she had," Tan explains, "about nine bad things that happened in our neighborhood and how we were doomed, that the deaths of my father and brother had to happen."

Much of what Tan had considered Chinese superstition, she later came to better understand and use in her two books, *The Joy Luck Club* and *The Kitchen God's Wife*. In her teens, however, Daisy Tan's Chinese ways were more of an embarrassment than anything else. Coupled with the pain of her

*In New York in 1993,
Ms. Tan wears a bracelet of
mahjong tiles, a gift from
one of the cast members
of* The Joy Luck Club.

father's and brother's deaths, Tan rebelled, seemingly fighting the world, and of course, her mother. She fell in with a crowd heavily involved with drugs. At 16, Tan was arrested for drug possession because some of her friends had been dealing hashish and psychedelics. "All those years of being good had done no good," Tan explained. "So I decided to be bad." At one point, she almost eloped to Australia with a German army deserter who had escaped from a mental hospital. Daisy Tan had the police go after Amy, and now Tan's response is: "Thank God! . . . It was the biggest drug bust in Montreux, Switzerland."

After graduating from high school in Switzerland, Tan attended Linfield College in McMinnville, Oregon, in

1969. There, she was to prepare for medical school. Within a year, however, she felt that there couldn't be a better life than reading, and decided to study English literature instead. "I remember [my mother] saying how disappointed my father would be," Amy recalls. "Chinese parents express their love by guiding their children . . . [and] I'd ignored my parents' wisdom."

Tan also met and fell in love with Louis DeMattie, who would later become her future husband. When Lou moved to California to attend San Jose State University, Amy went also, transferring to San Jose City College, and then later to San Jose State University. She received a B.A. with a double major in English and linguistics, and in 1974 an M.A. in linguistics. Tan then married Lou DeMattie, and in the two years to follow, she continued her education at the University of California at Santa Cruz, and U.C. Berkeley.

Though Amy had dreamed of becoming an artist or writer when she had been younger, she had also thought of it "as preposterous as a Chinese girl dreaming of becoming president of the United States." In her twenties and having graduated with a background in English did not make it any clearer to Tan that she was a writer. When she was eight, she had written an essay that won first prize in school. She received a transistor radio, and a local newspaper published her essay. In college she felt inspired by that memory, recognizing that she could still write essays well, but she had never taken any classes in creative writing.

Two years into her doctoral program at the University of California at Berkeley and her marriage to Lou, Tan started to feel the heavy burden of needing to know what she should do with her life at a time when she still wasn't sure. At the time, however, a close friend of her and her husband's was murdered during a robbery. "I had plenty of time to think," Tan has said. "Here was this person who had wonderful intentions to help other people and he was killed. And here I was doing crossword puzzles. What was I really doing with my life?"

Tan quit school at that point and went to work with disabled children. Though she loved this work, the emotional stress and frustration came to overwhelm her and eventually, after four years, she left. Soon, she had started freelance writing, eventually writing speeches for businesspeople at corporations such as AT&T, IBM, and Apple. This career was finally deemed a success by Daisy Tan because Amy was making a great deal of money. Tan was even able to buy her mother a house.

Her freelance work was demanding, however, and Tan found herself turning on the computer every day, reciting: "I hate it. I hate it. I hate it." But the more unhappy she was, the more she worked to try to force herself to be happy. When this strategy didn't work, Tan started to see a psychiatrist. He "fell asleep on three different occasions," she recalls.

Luckily, at that point, Tan started to read fiction again. One of the books she picked up and which became her favorite was *Love Medicine* by Louise Erdrich, a Native American writer of Chippewa descent. "What struck me about Erdrich was that her voice was unique," Tan has said. Other writers, she started to realize, also had that "irresistible" voice. Barbara Kingsolver, who is part Cherokee and author of the book *The Bean Trees,* is also, Tan believes, among the writers "outside the mainstream looking in and trying to adapt."

Tan started to wonder if perhaps she too had a "unique" writer's voice, and she suddenly got the feeling that she was really meant to write. Molly Giles, author of *Rough Translations* and leader of the writers' group that she joined, fed Tan the encouragement that she needed. In 1985, Amy completed her first story, "Rules of the Game," a story that was to become a part of *The Joy Luck Club.*

The Joy Luck Club was bought by a publisher in 1987, based on three such stories. Tan was given an advance of $50,000, and she worked every day from 8 A.M. to 7:30 P.M. When the book hit the stands in 1989, it became an instant

Authors Amy Tan and Dave Barry performing with their rock group, the Rock Bottom Remainders, at the 1992 American Booksellers Association convention in Anaheim, California.

best-seller. It focused on a series of mother-daughter relationships, the problems of miscommunication between the two generations, the past life of the mothers in China, and their lives with their daughters now in America. Perhaps it was only then that Tan began to understand her mother more clearly. "When I first wrote *Joy Luck Club,*" Tan explains, "it went on the *New York Times* best-seller list at number four, way beyond anything I ever expected. My mother said: 'Hmmm. Number four. Who is this number three? Number two? Number one?'" But Daisy Tan explained to her daughter that she wasn't disappointed, that "I just think you're so good that you always deserve to be number one."

Though her second book, *The Kitchen God's Wife,* is similar to the first in that it also focuses on a mother-daughter relationship, Tan holds that they are different stories. Starting a second book after her first had been such a success was difficult, and Tan had eight false starts. It was an idea of her mother's that Amy finally drew upon. Her mother told her: "Next book, write my true story." Tan did, and again, her second book became a best-seller.

Amy Tan's work was so well received by the American public that *The Joy Luck Club* was turned into a movie. Tan coproduced and cowrote it with the Oscar-winning writer Ron Bass, author of the screenplay for *Rain Man.* Directing the movie was the well-known Asian American director Wayne Wang, noted for movies such as *Eat a Bowl of Tea.* Wayne Wang had wanted to produce *The Joy Luck Club* because he felt strongly that they "could break down barriers for other Asian American artists." Tan, however, though she believes that the media ghettoizes Chinese Americans, felt that she didn't want the burden of that responsibility. "I don't feel that you can create rules about art, that you can't hire an actor that's less than fifty percent Asian," she explains, but "if they had wanted Debra Winger to dye her hair and paint her eyes, I would have been upset. It would have been insulting to the Chinese people." Many white actors have been chosen for Asian roles in movies and plays in the past. Tan comments that "it used to make me cringe."

On the less serious side, when Tan breaks out of her workaholic phases, she and a group of other writers, including Stephen King, Barbara Kingsolver, and David Barry, get together for the band that they have formed called the Rock Bottom Remainders. They tour together in a bus because, as Tan explains, "it's like summer camp. Nobody on the bus says, 'Where do you get your ideas?'" Though not pretending to be real musicians, they raise money for charities amidst morning food fights and Amy's singing "Leader of the Pack" dressed in S&M costume with whip in hand.

Tan has finally resolved the conflicts in her own relationship with her mother with the help of her first two books. She has written her story and her mother's as well. And though Tan did not go on to become a doctor the way her parents had originally planned, she has found success. Perhaps more important for Tan is the fact that "at the end of my life, if I was asked what the most important thing I did was, I would say: 'I made my mother happy.'"

Kimiko Hahn, photographed in 1988.

Kimiko
Hahn

OUIJA, THE BEATLES AND ROCK AND ROLL, BIKE RIDING, and reading were all things writer and poet Kimiko Hahn had fun doing. She always had friends, but at the same time she grew up feeling as if she were somehow caught "between poles ethnically and everything else." "It was hard because by being Eurasian in the United States, on the one hand," Kimiko explained, "you're not white and therefore, not considered American." But then, after her family had moved to Japan for a year, she found that she "wasn't white, so therefore not considered fully American, but also not Japanese."

Born on July 5, 1955, in Italy, Kimiko Hahn was the elder of two daughters of Walter and Maude Hamai Hahn. William Hahn was fourth-generation German American. Maude Hamai Hahn was second-generation Japanese American and grew up on the island of Maui in Hawaii where her parents were plantation workers. The Hahns met after the war. Maude Hamai Hahn went to Chicago Secretarial School in 1946 and later worked as a secretary in a school system, but her real love was arts and crafts such as macramé. Walter Hahn had been in the U.S. Navy. After the war, he went to study at the Art Institute of Chicago. Walter and Maude both took classes and lived at the YMCA. They became close friends and later married and settled in Pleasantville, a small suburb of New York. In 1955, Mr. Hahn, an art teacher and painter, won a major art award to study in Italy. There, Kimiko was born. After two years in Italy, the Hahns moved back to the suburbs of New York.

In Pleasantville, a town of 6,000 people, Kimiko, her mother, and her sister Tomiae were the few nonwhite people living there. "Part of the way we survived living out in the suburbs was that we kept going away," Kimiko said. At the age of eight, when Kimiko was still a Brownie with the Girl Scouts, her father took a year off from teaching and the family moved to Japan. There, Kimiko had many cousins and a sister to play with. She also learned to speak some Japanese and learned about Japanese culture.

The Hahns returned by boat and stopped at Hawaii to visit relatives. Then they circumnavigated the rest of the globe, stopping in Taiwan, Hong Kong, Thailand, Cambodia, India, Egypt, Portugal, and finally Italy. "I had quite an experience," Kimiko recalled, "My overall impression of the world was really very different outside the United States. People lived differently. I already knew that people spoke different languages. I knew that from the earliest point in my life because that was spent in Italy. People were always speaking different languages since I was a baby!" Kimiko also realized that it was important to respect different cultures and to be curious about them.

When the Hahns returned to the United States, Kimiko had a difficult time readjusting. After her best friend moved away, she began to feel more isolated. But because her parents had Kimiko take Japanese language and dance classes in New York City, Kimiko started to meet mostly Japanese American friends. "It was an outlet for me," she said. "It was really wonderful to have that whole world really tangent to my school world and my suburban life." Kimiko had always been an enthusiastic student, but she loved reading and writing the most. With the encouragement of a teacher and her mother, Kimiko started writing poetry in the third grade. "My mother would make little books out of paper," Kimiko re-called, "and I would draw the pictures and tell her the story and she would write the story down." Usually, these stories were about living in a tree house or running away to a fantasy island. These little storytelling episodes really built up Kimiko's confidence.

By the time she entered high school, Kimiko already knew that she wanted to be a writer. Writing and reading became an increasingly important part of her life. In English class, she read the works of Lawrence Ferlinghetti. "He was radical as far as I was concerned!" Kimiko recalled. e. e. cummings also impressed her. Kimiko spent her high school years practicing the craft of writing, and dating boys from New York City. Later, after college, she married one of her high school boyfriends, who was also Japanese American.

Home was recognizably different from her friends' houses, not so much because of her Japanese heritage, but because her parents were both artists. "My father especially is a bit eccentric," Kimiko said, mentioning that both her parents kept art projects all over the house. "A lot of our life was geared toward my father's artwork and the art world. So when we went on vacation, it was often to go to some city to see a museum." The Hahns also lived a very modest life, choosing travel and experiences that would enrich their lives over nice cars and a fancy house. "It was a very modest home because my parents really felt that it was more important to feed the mind."

Knowing that she wanted to be a writer when she graduated from high school in 1973, Kimiko went to the University of Iowa, which had a very strong writing program. There she wrote and studied with writers such as Louise Gluck, Marvin Bell, Charles Wright, and Michael Burkard. Missing the headiness of New York and her close friends, Kimiko took two years off during her junior year and returned to the city. During that period, she worked at a Japanese trading firm as a secretary. "But there's nothing like working to make you want to go back to school!" Kimiko said. Kimiko went back to Iowa and finished her program in three semesters, graduating in 1977.

Kimiko then returned to New York, where she married her longtime high school boyfriend. She worked briefly as a receptionist at the Asia Society while continuing to write in her free time. She enrolled in a graduate program in Japanese literature at Columbia University. "I was still serious about my writing, but I knew that it is really difficult to be an artist and make a living off of your art, especially poetry," Kimiko explained. "So I was trying to find some way to make a living. And I also wanted to learn Japanese." In graduate school, Kimiko read a great deal of Japanese short stories and poetry in translation, and later in Japanese as well. Though she didn't write very much, she found that her reading began to transform what she did write. Through classical Japanese writers such as Murasaki Shikibu and Sei Shonagon, as well as contemporary writers such as Kawabata, Kimiko came to be influenced by the form and content of Japanese writing. She came to appreciate the elegance and the devotion of these writers to imagery.

Again, there was a polarity in Kimiko's life: "Was I going to really devote myself to Japanese and Japanese studies and go live in Japan for a while? Or was I going to return to my own writing?" Ultimately, Kimiko said, "the best advice I got in graduate school was to go back to my own writing." After receiving her master's degree in Japanese literature, Kimiko concentrated on her poetry. Working three days a week as a research assistant for a professor of Japanese intel-

lectual history, Kimiko was able to make enough money to live while she started assembling her first book of poems. Her work for the professor was rewarding in many ways. She annotated books for the professor. "I loved that," Kimiko said. "And the professor was also a great inspiration to me, both as a female model, and also because of the kinds of things she was reading." Kimiko was in her late twenties and this was clearly one of the best times of her life. She could write, spend time with other artists, and work on different projects. In 1981, Kimiko went to West Virginia to work with a filmmaker on a project about coal miners and black lung disease.

It was also, however, in her late twenties that Kimiko divorced her husband. Though they were and continue to be good friends, the couple had been drifting apart and the breakup became inevitable. Kimiko was heavily active in an

The Hahn family in 1975. Kimiko's parents, Walter Hahn and Maude Hamai Hahn, met at the Art Institute of Chicago in the 1950s. She is very close to her sister, Tomiae.

organization called Artists Against U.S. Intervention in Central America. It was through this organization that Kimiko met Ted Hannan, her present husband, whom she married three years later. In 1982, Kimiko traveled twice to Nicaragua. "I was interested in what the artist's role was under the Sandinistas. It was thrilling to be there and to see artists participate in society and not be marginalized as they are in the United States," Kimiko said. "Not to be treated special or be treated as oddities, but as a part of everyday life and what people do."

Daughters Miyako, born in 1985, and Reiko, born in 1988, forced Kimiko to compartmentalize her life in terms of making special time for her writing, family, and herself. "Sometimes one would try to pull away from the other and I've increasingly learned to relax more and be able to devote myself to what I'm doing at the moment," Kimiko explained, "So when I'm with my children, it's not time to write. And when it's time to write, it's time to write." The family spends time together going to places like the library or the pet shop, and they love artistic performances and roller-skating!

Air Pocket, Kimiko's first book of poetry, was published in 1989. These poems were written primarily when she was in her twenties. Some of the poems had already appeared in an anthology of three women poets entitled *We Stand Our Ground.* Kimiko also started teaching at Sarah Lawrence College and became a visiting professor at Yale and Barnard for several semesters. *Earshot,* a second volume of poetry, was published in 1992. Its poems focus on themes of betrayal and jealousy. Kimiko here uses themes and images taken from *The Tale of Genji* by the Japanese writer Murasaki Shikibun. There are also poems about her two daughters.

Currently, Kimiko works as an assistant professor of English at Queens College, which is part of the City University of New York. Her third book, *Unbearable Heart,* to be published by Kaya Press, is a collection of poetry that focuses on her mother's death as a result of a car accident. Kimiko is now writing her fourth collection of poetry, which will be more political than personal. Two poems to be included date back to her experience with coal miners and black lung disease in West Virginia and her time in Nicaragua. "It will be more outward looking," Kimiko says, "the world outside my home."

Kimiko is also working on a collection of prose and some children's stories. On the days that she doesn't teach, she does the three things she loves best: writing, reading, and aerobics. When her schedule allows, she also enjoys getting together with other writers to talk about what they are doing. But these days, though Kimiko's life has always been filled with different levels of polarities, it is clear that writing is a vocation to which she has remained faithful.

Li-Young Lee

IT IS MIDAFTERNOON, BUT LI-YOUNG MUST SNEAK OUT of his house with his brother and the family cook, Ah Sey, who takes them to a Cantonese noodle house in Hong Kong to enjoy their favorite noodles with spicy chili sauce. If his father, a popular but strict Baptist minister, knew they'd left the safety of the house at all, they'd really be in trouble. But he's away preaching on this day, so they can be free, and how would he ever know anyway? They just have to be careful to go straight to the restaurant, eat, and then go right home. On the way, the group sees colored fliers strewn across the street. It is a beautiful sight. Li-Young picks one up. Surprisingly, it is a picture of his father with the time and date that he will preach. It hits Li-Young for the first time, exactly how popular a preacher his father really is. Somehow, his father's presence is everywhere.

Today, close to 30 years later, Li-Young recalls such moments in his two books of poetry, *Rose* and *The City in Which I Love You*. These books have both received New York University's Delmore Schwartz Memorial Poetry Award and have been included in the 1990 Lamont Poetry Selection of the Academy of American Poets. One critic called Li-Young a "natural" poet, "one whose growth will be a thing of beauty."

Li-Young Lee was born in 1957 in Jakarta, Indonesia. His father, Lee Guo Yuan, and mother, Yuan Jia Ying, had come from Tianjin, China, sometime after the Communists took power and the Nationalists fled to Taiwan. For nine months, Li-Young's father was personal physician to Communist leader Mao Zedong, until political conditions forced him to flee with his wife to Jakarta in 1951, leaving behind a son with his maternal grandparents.

In Jakarta, Guo Yuan took the opportunity to pursue his dream of establishing a genuine school for spiritual questioning. He taught philosophy at Gamaliel University, an intellectual institution that would attract Western theologians. Guo Yuan's program ranged from reading philosophy to basic mission work feeding the poor, who included mainly Indonesians and Chinese. His father, obsessed with the Old Testament, had taught himself Hebrew. "It was a new spirituality that he didn't understand," Li-Young explains. "It's a religion of the injured and insulted, which dealt with human pain, but where man and God are one." For the Lees, who were forced to flee their own country, such a religion offered solace and hope. Settled in their new home, they had two children, one of whom was Li-Young.

The situation in Indonesia, however, took a bad turn in 1954 when President Sukarno announced a purge of all Chinese resident aliens. In the following years, Li-Young's father was sent as a political prisoner to a leper colony for his involvement with the university, but he managed to sneak away. "It was a miraculous escape," Li-Young points out. His father lived like a fugitive for the next ten years, constantly assuming different names while on the run with his family, traveling first to Macao and Hong Kong, then to Japan, Singapore, and then back to Japan.

With the constant culture shock and feeling of displacement after each move, it became clear to Li-Young that "home" would never be a fixed geographic place with the same friends and familiar places. Where was home? It was supposed to be China, though Li-Young was not born there. He was born in Indonesia, but he had been forced to flee. Was his home in Hong Kong, Macao, Singapore, or Japan? Or was it all of these places? Does home move when you do? His parents thought of themselves as Chinese. They could recite by heart Chinese Sung and Tang dynasty poetry. Li-Young's father, a man that he both "loved and feared," was so moved by these poems that he would openly weep in front of his children. "I really got to see how literature was a lifeline for him," Li-Young explains. Though at the time literature meant the Bible his father forced him to read, literature would become a lifeline for Li-Young too. For him, language would become a homeland, though not a physical, biological home. Li-Young would one day believe so firmly in a homeland in the language of English that English would become vital to his life.

Li-Young's parents tried to impress on their children the importance of memories. They often told their children romantic stories, trying to give them a sense of roots, even if they were speaking about a place they didn't know, because that place might have been "home" had circumstances been different. When asked if his parents had a traditionally arranged marriage, Li-Young replied "No, they met out of love and married." Though the story of their meeting varied depending on whether his mother or father told it, he remembers a version that is something between both. "They got married but then war broke out and he went off to war. (My mother's) father made her get a divorce in case (my father) got killed. So they got divorced," Li-Young says tragically. "But she locked herself in a room for a year and a half until he came back."

Another "crazy" story that Li-Young grew up with was the story about the uncle who fell in love with his niece. Because he wasn't allowed to marry her, he gave up his inheritance and went off to Tibet. "He wrote love letters back to his niece," Li-Young says. "I have a picture of him with his hair long and white, sitting on a horse. And he's writing love poems for her!"

Perhaps it was these stories that helped to keep the family united during this period of crisis. Li-Young's parents knew a constantly growing number of friends who had been tortured and killed by the Indonesian authorities. Li-Young's father turned increasingly toward the Bible to keep himself sane, and more importantly, to keep his faith. Li-Young would look back on this lonely period and remember singular moments, such as the arrival in Hong Kong. "Looking out the boat window and seeing the Hong Kong shore . . . my parents laughing in the other room . . . the diapers hanging up in the room. We were in third class because only the British and the Americans were allowed in first and second class. There were dirty diapers everywhere. It smelled bad."

Fortunately, the Lees were finally able to immigrate in 1964 to the United States. They settled in Pennsylvania, where Li-Young's father was accepted at the Pittsburgh Theological Society. "My parents were poor but it was a great time," Li-Young recalls. The family got their first Christmas tree, and the children went to school. It was in school that Li-Young learned to get tough. "It was a working-class community," Li-Young explains, after describing how he was a "brute" with a shaved head who wore safety pins in his chest. "The last time (the community) saw an Asian was during the wars when they were shooting at the Japanese." Forced to cope with the racism and verbal insults, Li-Young led a schizophrenic existence between acting the tough guy and satisfying his growing love for poetry. "It's kind of embarrassing,"

Li-Young admits, laughing. "When I was in high school, I found Robert Louis Stevenson's *A Child's Garden of Verses*. I thought they were the most beautiful things in the world. It was really sappy!"

Throughout school, Li-Young continued to show the world the face of one person, while internally he felt he was another. When he went to college at the University of Pittsburgh, he began for the first time to write his own poetry. He loved Robert Frost and Walt Whitman as well as contemporary poets such as Carruth and Roethke. Later, he would come upon Garrett Hongo, also an Asian American writer. After reading Hongo's collection of poems in *The River of Heaven*, Li-Young says he felt "so happy" and "so proud." Later, he would discover many other Asian American writers and poets that he would come to love, such as Wendy Law-Yone, Marilyn Chin, and Lois-Ann Yamanaka.

By the age of 20, Li-Young had his own romantic love story to tell. Donna Bozzarelli was an Italian girl he had known since they were in the fifth grade together. Donna was a parishioner of the church where Li-Young's father was minister in Pennsylvania. The two had shared a close friendship as children. When they grew older, the relationship, as Li-Young explains, turned "erotic." They married and had two sons, Shyu Tang, born in 1984, and Yu Tang, in 1985. Li-Young enjoys playing with them, reading to them, and especially eating with them.

When he graduated with a bachelor of arts from Pittsburgh, Li-Young and his brothers opened a restaurant. "I was writing poetry and flipping burgers for a year," Li-Young says with a laugh. When the luncheonette went bankrupt after a year, however, Li-Young went back to school. He was accepted into the master of fine arts program for writing at the University of Arizona. He wasn't happy there, and after a year he had flunked out. "The timing was wrong," he adds. "I just went bankrupt and my father was dying." Later, his father's death would provide a doorway for Li-Young to explore. "I was always obsessed about death," Li-Young explains, "but I needed a concrete door into that subject. And my father was that door because he was dying as long as I knew him. After prison, he was dying."

After Li-Young's father died, he returned to graduate school at the State University of New York at Brockport. Again, he went for a year and then decided that he would rather educate himself by reading. He read more and more books, averaging five books a week while working in a Chicago warehouse. "I put myself on a regimen of three hours' sleep, 14 cups of coffee to stay awake," Lee explained. Though he had already published some of his work in a magazine in 1979, he stopped publishing altogether to concentrate fully on his writing. He was writing more poetry than ever before and he was also reading heavily in philosophy, theology, psychology, and fiction. He lived with this regimen for close to five years, waiting for something "divine" to happen. What happened instead was that his health gave way and he just collapsed on his living room floor. At that point, he realized that "my bravado about poetry being divine was a fear of having other people see it."

Li-Young altered his lifestyle and soon published the poetry collection entitled *Rose*, which received positive reviews and which also won him a $20,000 fellowship from the National Endowment for the Arts. At that point, Li-Young was able to quit his warehouse job to write full-time. The

outcome was *The City in Which I Love You*, published in 1990.
In this book, there is a poem called "The Cleaving," which
makes reference to Emerson, who had written that the Chinese:

> . . . *managed to preserve to the hair*
> *for three or four thousand years*
> *the ugliest features in the world.*

Li-Young's responded with:

> *I would eat these features, eat*
> *the last three or four thousand years, every hair.*
> *And I would eat Emerson, his transparent soul, his*
> *soporific transcendence.*

"I wasn't surprised or hurt," Li-Young clarifies. "I
just thought. 'You're a man, too, a human being.'" But what
Li-Young did feel, at that point, was a feeling of estrangement
from within the language. Here was a language he loved that
had insulted him. "Language had been used against my kind,"
Li-Young explains. "Yet I'm intelligent enough to know that
there's enough of Emerson that I deeply love that that remark
doesn't sum everything up."

Confronting racism brought Li-Young into a very
complex relationship with literature and, more broadly, the
whole culture. "I started having these feelings that if I could
change a reader's idea of our meaning and value, then I could
change their habits of thought." He adds, "It's our habits of
thinking that make us racist, or sexist, all that stuff." Li-
Young would like to change all of that through his poetry. "I
want to change them," he says, "I want to adjust their thought
patterns." To Li-Young, reading poetry is a spiritual practice.

And writing poetry is an even greater spiritual practice. "Poetry captures a moment like a glimpse. . . . It is the only reality. . . . What is real? Only this, this consciousness. And poetry is about consciousness."

For Li-Young, what this means is that his poetry must explore his origins. Origins that have to do with who he is, that go beyond the boundaries of China or wherever he comes from. He writes in order to be right there at the moment of creation. It is an enactment of a vision. He goes so far as to say: "It is not even a matter of my writing poetry or not writing poetry. . . . I would like to overthrow poetry." He would like to close in on the origins of language, and yet, because each individual has his or her own differing "reality," the more he feels he comes closer to those origins, the more people he feels his poetry loses.

Most recently, Li-Young has focused less of his time on his poetry and turned his attention toward a personal memoir. "I thought it would be easy," he explains, "but then it occurred to me that I was somehow talking about things that are nearest and dearest to me. And anything that dear to me deserves to be written in poetry because poetry is eternal." It will live on, he believes, as a personal myth, a kind of journey or passage. "Not the other person's passage, not your father's passage, not your mother's passage. Not all the fathers' passages in history. It's my passage."

This boy who grew up and journeyed halfway across the world to find his "home," discovered no geographical place but a language that he loves and creates in his poems. But writing is often a tough job. Even now, with 20 years of writing experience and two successful books of poetry behind him, Li-Young has his moments of doubt. "I don't think I'm a poet yet," he says. "I'm still waiting for it. One of these days God is going to come down and kiss me on the back of the head. And then I'll have a poem."

For his readers, however, the poems are already there, and as poet and critic Frederick Smock has pointed out, Li-Young's poems "unfold, like a rose, seemingly without effort. And yet effortlessness is not achieved without great talent and diligence." And nothing can take that creative gift away from him.

Maxine Hong Kingston in front of the Portland Theater in 1993.

"I HAVE NO IDEA HOW PEOPLE WHO DON'T WRITE EN-dure their lives," Maxine Hong Kingston has remarked. By the age of 15, she had already begun exploring issues of identity that would preoccupy her writing throughout adult-hood. She had written an essay about her experiences as a young Chinese American woman, entitling it "I Am an Ameri-can." Later, in her first book, *The Woman Warrior*, she wrote "Better to raise geese than girls." And in her later books, *China Men* and *Tripmaster Monkey*, she continues to speak out about sexism and racism as she mixes and weaves myths and folklore, the Chinese and English languages, and "missing" parts of Asian American history into her narratives. In her writing, she also draws on her personal experience of growing up Chinese American, the lives of her parents as immigrants, and family secrets and stories about "ghosts" and the past "better left forgotten." Through the Chinese American protagonists in her books, she has exposed painful truths and discovered a powerful voice as a novelist.

Maxine Hong was born on October 27, 1940, in Stockton, California. Her father had been a scholar and teacher in his village near Guangzhou, China. Though teach-ing was considered a prestigious job, Maxine's father left China for America, seeking a better future. He left Ying Lan, his wife, and their two children, and settled in New York, renaming himself Tom after Thomas Edison. Working in a laundry, it took 15 years for him to save enough money to send for his family. During the years of separation, however, both children died. At a time when few women in China were educated, Ying Lan decided to study medicine and midwifery.

Afterward, she set up her own practice in a small village called Sun Woi. When Ying Lan finally joined Tom in New York in her late thirties, they moved and settled in Stockton, California. Tom found a job as a manager at a gambling house. Ying Lan worked as field help or in the canneries. The first of six children they would have in America, Maxine was named after a blond woman who frequented the gambling house and who had the good fortune of always winning. Her parents hoped that Maxine would have the same luck.

The Hongs eventually bought their own laundry and it became a family business in which each member had to participate. There was more than enough washing, drying, and pressing for the parents and their six children. While at the laundry, Maxine listened to her mother "talk story." These tales stemmed from an oral tradition handed down from one generation to another. They were a mixture of anecdotes, legends, and ghost tales. Maxine would later incorporate some of these stories into her books. One such story from ancient China was about Fa Mu Lan, a woman who disguises herself as a man in order to take her father's place in the army. She leaves for battle and eventually returns a powerful and respected general. Maxine Hong Kingston later used this legend as an emblem for her own life as a Chinese American woman feminist in *The Woman Warrior.*

Young Maxine was a very quiet girl during her first years in school. At home, her parents only spoke a dialect of Chinese, and she had no exposure to English until she entered school. As she grew a little older, she found that she could not speak above a "duck's quack." She did, however, articulate her stories in drawings that she covered over with black ink.

Though at the time her teachers thought Maxine was intentionally trying to destroy her pictures, Maxine had actually been covering these scenes with curtains. She envisioned her drawings as plays or operas that were about to happen. It was that momentary peak of anticipation that Maxine tried the most to capture, as if it were she who stood behind that curtain eagerly awaiting life to begin.

Maxine describes her young self as studious and quiet, but she always loved to tell stories. At home and at Chinese school, she felt free to speak out, and by doing so nurtured her storytelling ability. She remembers various stories she created at the age of eight or nine and how these stories were, perhaps, the first stages of what would eventually evolve into her second book, *China Men.* She also remembers that she always wanted to be a writer, that she loved telling stories and writing them down. Her mother's "talk story" tradition helped Maxine to listen and to develop her own style of storytelling and writing.

At an early age, Maxine fell in love with books. She remembers a bad experience, however, after having read *Little Women* by Louisa May Alcott. While reading this book, Maxine had identified herself with the beautiful protagonist, Jo March. At one point, however, Jo is in the midst of describing a Chinese man as: "short and fat, and wadded comically; his eyes were very slanting . . . his queue was long, so were his nails, his yellow face was plump and shiny, and he was altogether a highly satisfactory Chinaman." Reading this description made Maxine feel as if she were betrayed by a close friend. Literature had been a haven for her, but the ugliness in those words left her "pushed out," an ugly "Chinaman."

Luckily, Maxine continued to read, soon coming upon *Fifth Chinese Daughter* by another Chinese American woman, Jade Snow Wong. Maxine Hong Kingston recalls how this book "saved my life" because it restored her faith in literature, and more important, her self-esteem.

Maxine enrolled at the University of California at Berkeley in 1958. Though her math skills were excellent and it was expected that she would pursue engineering as a career, Maxine couldn't ignore her calling to write. By her second year, she had switched her major accordingly. This change had a positive effect on her. By the time she graduated in 1962, she had been awarded 11 scholarships that had enabled her to finish college. While at Berkeley, she appeared in Bertolt Brecht's play *Galileo,* where she met another actor, Earll Kingston, and they married soon after Maxine graduated. Their son, Joseph, was born in 1963. Right after college, Maxine took a job teaching at a high school in Hayward, California.

During the 1960s, however, Maxine and Earll took part in the protest movement against the war in Vietnam, joining the Universal Life Church, where they soon became ordained ministers. As the violence increased and Maxine and Earll felt more alienated by the war, they decided they had no choice but to leave the country. They had intended to move to Japan, but on their way there, they stopped over in Hawaii. Ultimately, they stayed in Hawaii for the next 17 years! There, Maxine taught at various public and private schools while Earll worked at a Shakespearean theater. She also began writing *The Woman Warrior* and *China Men*, both written in the "talk story" tradition.

"You're leading the life that I wanted," Maxine's father told Maxine after he read *China Men.* He was proud to have had Maxine live out some of his own dreams as a writer and scholar. "Father, I'm going to write your stories, and you'll just have to speak up if I've got you wrong," Maxine had told him. As traditional scholars would have done, Mr. Hong wrote commentaries for both *China Men* and *The Woman Warrior* in the margins of each manuscript. Maxine has noted how her father's comments were reconciling, especially in sections of *The Woman Warrior* where there was a great deal of angry feminist accusation. "Women hold up half the sky," he would comment, leaving similar proverbs etched into the manuscript. To surprise her father, Maxine arranged to have the manuscripts with his commentary displayed at the Bancroft Library. There, during the opening reception, her father went straight up to the display. "My writing," he said in English, a proud smile across his face.

Maxine has said that the power of her style comes from the way people such as her parents actually speak, that the music in the writing often comes from vocabulary that people invent or reinvent in place of words they do not know. Maxine has attributed her style to her Chinese American voice: the way she has acquired and adapted the storytelling tradition her mother handed down to her, and also the actual usage of language—both English and Chinese—in her stories.

The Woman Warrior was to become what many writers dream of. Accepted for publication almost immediately, the book also became an instant critical success. It won the 1976 National Book Critics Circle Award for nonfiction and became a best-seller. She received a number of major awards, including the *Mademoiselle* magazine award, the Anisfield-Wolf Race Relations Award, as well as a fellowship from the National Endowment for the Arts. In 1980, she received the

Maxine Hong Kingston and her husband, Earll Kingston, on the site of their Oakland house, which burned to the ground in the summer of 1992. The manuscript of her fourth novel was lost in the fire.

National Book Award for nonfiction for her second book, *China Men.*

Interestingly, when asked in interviews if there were any changes that she wished to make in her books, Maxine has responded affirmatively. In *The Woman Warrior,* Maxine reinterpreted the legend of Fa Mu Lan. In a more traditional version, Fa Mu Lan returns to her village as a general leading her army. Once at home, she changes out of her warrior garb and into her flowing robes. She does her hair, puts flowers into it, then presents herself to the soldiers in her command. Fa Mu Lan reveals her feminine beauty. When writing *The Woman Warrior,* Maxine Hong Kingston deliberately left out that part of the story. As a feminist, she wanted to get rid of the high-heeled shoes, the makeup, and the other things that trapped women within the feminine image. But now she wishes that she could have reconciled those parts of the heroine's story. A woman could have both those powers; she could leave for war and return whole and not brutalized.

Though *The Woman Warrior* is an ideal that Maxine is constantly striving to reach, her pacifism has continued to grow and now she wishes that she had not chosen a title with the word *warrior* in it. She no longer believes that war is an appropriate metaphor for her struggle. She believes that writers should exhibit a kind of modesty and try to conquer one reader at a time with their visions. Though she sees herself up against people with enormous power, she believes that the words are more powerful because they can change minds. "Ultimately," Kingston has said, books will prevail because "power comes from the heart and the mind."

Tripmaster Monkey and the book she is currently working on both revolve around the protagonist Whittman Ah Sing, a fifth-generation Chinese American male. Whittman, like Maxine, was a Berkeley graduate living the 1960s experience. His interests are also in writing and theater and Maxine has said in interviews that had she been born a man, she would have liked to be like Whittman. He is a jester trying to change the world with his tricks and laughter. Whittman is an incessant talker, with a great deal to say and no fear of doing so. Like Maxine, he is a believer in peace, a writer trying to save the world in more powerful ways than the bullet. He is truly American, in the sense that he tries to search for his roots in his community, though his strong sense of individualism keeps him alienated from his "people." There have been Chinese American men who have responded to Maxine: "You must have been following me around, that's my life." One such man is Frank Chin, a playwright and founder of the San Francisco Asian American Theater Company. He has claimed that Whittman Ah Sing is a portrait of himself. Maxine has responded that Whittman was a combination of several people, as well as herself.

In 1987, a collection of 11 of Kingston's stories, which originally appeared in the "Hers" column of the *New York Times,* was published as a limited edition under the title *Hawai'i One Summer.* In the finest bookmaking tradition, careful attention was paid to all materials from paper and ink to the leather of the binding. "This incarnation of my pieces has surprised me," Maxine responded, "there is such an honoring, loving, preserving of the writing . . .[an] opposite treatment from the disposable, ephemeral, accessible nature of a newspaper column."

Maxine returned to teaching English at Berkeley. Her fourth book, the sequel to *Tripmaster Monkey,* was to bring Whittman up to date as a grown man. Unfortunately, the entire manuscript was destroyed in the Oakland fire during the summer of 1992. Confronted with this frustrating and heartbreaking mishap, Maxine asked herself what her options were. Should she try to rewrite the novel from memory, or should she just give it up and move on to a new writing project? She decided that the only way to save herself was to save her writing. Currently, Maxine remains in seclusion somewhere near the Grand Canyon as she tackles the rewrite of her fourth novel.

David Mura.

THE YEAR WAS 1959. THE CHICAGO WHITE SOX WERE competing against the Los Angeles Dodgers in the World Series. David Mura was seven years old when his father picked him up early from school and together they headed for Comiskey Park. The Sox were in the lead, 1–0, 2–0, 3–0, inning after inning, until finally they won with a score of 11–0! Though they would later lose four games in a row and lose the series, this game would always be remembered as magical for David. His team had won and he had been there. It would always be one of the happiest moments in his life.

Writer and poet David Mura was born on June 17, 1952, in Great Lakes, Illinois. He is Sansei, meaning that he is third-generation Japanese American. His father, Tom, had shortened his family name from Uemura to Mura sometime after World War II. It was during the war that Tom spent his high school years in an internment camp. David's mother, Teruko Nakauchi, was also at a camp. The couple met later, at a Nisei (second-generation) dance sometime after the war and the camps. Both families had moved to Chicago to start their lives anew. They met and then married in 1951. David was one of four siblings. For a while, the Muras lived in the city, where they were active in a church whose congregation was made up of Japanese American families like themselves.

Life changed for David when he was nine and his parents moved out into the suburbs. He had Japanese American friends, but on the whole the community was white, so most of his friends were white as well. For his parents, this was the dream they'd been looking for. It was a chance to live "American" lives and forget about a painful past. They spoke English at home and though David had to follow certain customs like taking his shoes off at the door, he always figured

David Mura

it was because his mom had white carpets. "We raised you to be an individual first, and an American second, but not Japanese. Maybe that was wrong," his parents have told him only recently. At the time, they never talked about their experiences in the internment camps, and when David asked them about it, his mother would always reply, "I was too young to remember." And his father explained, "When I was younger in Los Angeles, I used to have to work in my father's nursery every day after school. When I got to the camps, I got to go out every day to play baseball." But for David's parents, the internment was a painful experience, one that they wanted to erase and were reluctant to talk about. "One of the ways I think about this experience is that if you are put in prison for being a shoplifter and you want to show people that you are reformed, you don't shoplift any more," David explained about his parents. "So what happens when you're put in prison for being of Japanese ancestry? You try not to be Japanese any more."

For David, the transition to a new school wasn't as difficult as it could have been for others because he was one of the biggest baseball and football fans around. He was also athletic and great at all the sports he played. "Being good at sports is helpful," David says, thinking back. "I had a certain amount of acceptance." His involvement on different teams quickly made him very popular at school. David thought, read about, and lived for sports. At one point, his mother complained because David also "talked like a jock." His favorite books were about sports or sports figures, though sometimes he also enjoyed reading biographies of different presidents. "When I was in third grade," David remembers, "I wanted to be either the president or the janitor. I wanted to be president because you ran the country, and I wanted to be janitor because the janitor in our building got to throw coal into the furnace. And it was the big furnace with flames shooting out of it."

David was to become neither president nor janitor. Instead, he was to pursue a career as a writer and poet. David would never have thought so, then. His skills in math and social sciences were always much better than his writing and English skills. David had written some of his first poems in high school, but his father was extremely critical about anything he wrote. One poem was about a boy in the ghetto sitting by his window. "My father yelled at me," Mura says now, laughing. "He yelled: 'Why don't you write about what you know?'" As a result, David didn't start writing poetry again until he went away to college.

Another pressure that affected him during high school was the dating scene. On one occasion David's intramural basketball team won the league championship. His team went on to play the intramural all-stars and beat them too. Before the game, David remembers having talked with one of his friends about a party that someone was having the following night. "Wouldn't it be great if we won?" David said. He was the star of the game, but he found that once he got to the party with his friends, he wasn't the star of the party and he wasn't considered one of the attractive people there, either. It was difficult because David felt isolated with no one to talk to. Was he not attractive or was it because he was Japanese, he wondered. "Is it me?" His teens were a particularly painful time for David, and from that point on, he was constantly trying to disassociate himself from stereotypes of the quiet, studious, and nerdy Asian student. By the time he entered high school, he had developed a loud and obnoxious personality to ward off the stereotype. "I ended up being the best-dressed in my high school and I think I dressed that way in part to say, 'Look! I'm not going to dress the way the "nerds" dress,'" David explains. "And all the time I did that, the stereotype was still controlling me." He felt trapped. "Nowhere in my mind did I associate being Japanese with anything positive."

David graduated from high school and went to Grinnell College. There, everyone seemed busy songwriting. "It was the era of people like James Taylor, Bob Dylan, and Neil Young," David explains, "so I started writing myself." He also took a class in major English poets that changed his career plans. He had planned to become a lawyer, but after he did an excellent job on an assignment to write imitations of the poetry of Spenser and Pope, he decided to become an English major. From that point on, David started to write.

After graduating with honors in 1974, David went on to graduate school at the University of Minnesota. In the English program there, David learned more about classic English literature, reading authors such as Browning, Donne, Shakespeare, Eliot, and Faulkner. Among his favorite contemporary poets were Robert Lowell, John Berryman, and Randall Jarrell. Later, he identified with writers such as James Griden and Philip Levine. "I went through an English program in college, five years of English in graduate school, and the only work by a writer of color I ever read was a handful of poems by Baraka," David notes. "The message was that 'minority writing' was a literary ghetto or 'minor league stuff.'" David knew he needed to confront his own identity as a Japanese American poet. He dropped out of graduate school with five incompletes and entered intensive therapy to deal with these unresolved issues. At the time, though he hadn't yet come to think of himself as an Asian American poet, he was already writing more and more about what it meant to be Japanese. Many of his poems focused on his grandfather, the internment camps, the *hibakusha* (victims of the atomic bomb), or his uncle who fought with the all-Japanese 442nd Regimental Combat Team during the war.

In 1984, David won the U.S.–Japan Creative Arts Exchange Fellowship. He accepted, but honestly admitted that he would have liked to study in Paris; preferring Baudelaire and Proust over Basho or Kawabata. He left for a year in Japan with his wife, Susan Sencer, a pediatric oncologist and longtime friend from college whom he married in 1983. His stay in Japan would change his outlook on himself and on the world. The journal he kept, which documented his observations and feelings about Japanese culture, eventually evolved into *Turning Japanese: Memoirs of a Sansei*. The book explores his identity as a Japanese American. "Japan allowed me to see myself, America, and the world from a perspective that was not white American," he explains in the book. Immersed in Japanese culture, David started taking Japanese language lessons and was welcomed into an apprenticeship in Noh singing and Buto dance. He thought he "might actually become part of that country." For once, he could walk the streets and not stand out as looking different. More importantly, however, his time in Japan gave him the chance to appreciate the complexities of Japanese culture and the richness of its history.

David returned to the United States the following year and his writing now reflected a reaffirmation of pride in being Japanese American. He also began to think of himself as an Asian American writer, and a writer of color. "My struggle with identity is here, not in Japan," he said. In 1985, David won a fellowship from the National Endowment for the Arts. He continued writing and went on to a master of fine arts program at the University of Vermont, graduating in 1991. During that period, he published his first book, *A Male Grief: Notes on Pornography and Addiction* in 1989, and then a book of poetry, *After We Lost Our Way*, in 1989. His memoir, *Turning Japanese*, came out in 1991. Since then, he has returned to the Twin Cities and has been working to support the Asian American arts community in the Twin Cities. He has served as a board member for the Asian American Renaissance Conference. This activity brought David closer to other Asian American writers such as Garrett Hongo, Marilyn Chin, Li-Young Lee, and Frank Chin. Many of these writers have come to influence him and his writing. "I don't think our aesthetics are very close," David says about writer Garrett Hongo, "but it's very clear when I talk to him that we share a lot of things about our experiences, and the depth with which we are able to talk about certain issues is a depth that I'm not able to reach with a lot of people."

These days, David juggles his time between various community activities, the business part of being a writer, the actual writing, and his family. He has two children, Samantha, born in 1989, and son Nikko, born in 1994. "I'm aware that my kids are only going to be this age very briefly and so they're in day care three to four days a week and then I have one or two days a week for my writing," David says. The zoo is a place the three like to frequent together.

David has just completed a show with a friend called *The Colors of Desire*. It is a multimedia piece involving live music,

video, and animation. The work deals with African American
and Asian American relationships. The authors are also now
working on a small film for PBS which will focus on some of
the same themes. *The Colors of Desire,* another book of poetry,
is to be published in 1995, and David has already started a
second memoir. This book will cover the first half of his life.

When asked why he became a writer, David has one
response: "So I wouldn't get bored. Because it's always chang-
ing and it constantly seems impossible. There is an intrinsic
pleasure I get in writing which has to do with the pleasure of
tackling the problem of articulating your life and the way you
look at the world. . . . On a different level, writing is to escape
the limitations of your own self. Or to attempt to, though I
don't think you ever actually do." Writing for David will
always remain a challenge, at times an extremely painful one,
but it is a challenge he can't ignore.

Michael Ondaatje.

TYPICALLY, IT'S A NOVELIST'S JOB TO BRING TOGETHER all the facts that will determine the actions and the fate of his characters. For Michael Ondaatje, poet, playwright, novelist, and filmmaker, the process of collating information is quite different. For him, the fewer facts there are, the more there is to explore. "I knew very little," Michael explained about a real-life character he fictionalized in one of his novels. "I'm really drawn to unfinished stories. There's all those empty spaces you can put stuff in."

Philip Michael Ondaatje was born on September 12, 1943, in Ceylon, now called Sri Lanka. His paternal grandfather was a wealthy tea planter with a large family estate in Kegalle. His father, Philip Mervyn Ondaatje, had been sent by his parents to England to study at university. Two and a half years later, his parents discovered that he hadn't even passed the entrance exam and had instead been living extravagantly off the money that they had sent him. To escape his parents' wrath, he announced his engagement to one of his sister's close friends. His parents were satisfied until Mervyn announced only four months before the wedding that the engagement was off—that he was to marry instead Doris Gratiaen, his best friend's sister. Doris Gratiaen was a dancer, and later ran a small theater and dance school. The couple married in May 1932 and settled in Ceylon. Michael was the youngest of their four children.

Though his parents divorced when Michael was only five, he points out in his autobiography, *Running in the Family*, that they were perfect for each other. In a photograph taken during their honeymoon, his father sits facing the camera while his mother faces him so that she is in profile. "My

Michael Ondaatje

father's pupils droop to the southwest corner of his sockets. His jaw falls and resettles into a groan that is half idiot, half shock. . . . My mother in white has twisted her lovely features and stuck out her jaw and upper lip so that her profile is in the posture of a monkey." This photograph was made into postcards that read on the back: "What we think of married life." They shared the same sense of humor. What separated them after close to 16 years were Mervyn's severe bouts with alcoholism. They divorced in 1948. Doris didn't ask for alimony or child support. To support herself and the schooling of her children, she started working as a housekeeper-manager in various Ceylon hotels. Later, when she moved to England in 1949, she would continue to work in hotels as well.

After the divorce, Michael's father returned to his father's estate in Kegalle and took up chicken farming. Though Michael was away at St. Thomas College, he spent holidays with his father on the estate. By 1950, Mervyn had remarried. Two years later, when Michael was 11, he joined his mother in England. It would be 26 years before Michael would return to Sri Lanka. He would never meet his father again. "My loss was that I never spoke to him as an adult," Michael wrote. "Was he locked in the ceremony of being a 'father'? He died before I even knew of such things."

In England, Michael attended Dulwich College. At 19, he immigrated to Montreal, Canada, to join his brother. There, he attended Bishop's University in Quebec, majoring in English and history. One of his teachers, Arthur Motyer, encouraged Michael to start writing. Michael read avariciously, influenced by poets such as Browning, Eliot, and Yeats, as well as many of the younger modern poets such as

D. G. Jones. After two years, Michael transferred to the University of Toronto where he received his bachelor of arts degree in 1965.

It was in 1964 that Michael married artist and filmmaker Kim Jones. Together, they had two children, Quentin in 1966, and Griffin in 1965. From Kim's previous marriage, they had an additional four children in their lively household.

The first of Michael's poetry to be published appeared in 1966 in *New Wave Canada,* an anthology of young poets. He then went on to obtain his master of arts degree at Queen's University in 1967. By the time he obtained his degree, he had won the Epstein Award for poetry, bringing him to the attention of Coach House Press. It was with this small but influential press that Michael published his first book of poetry, *The Dainty Monsters,* in 1967. Reviewers loved the startling imagery, and for a first book of poetry, it was very well received.

In the same year that *The Dainty Monsters* was published, Michael started teaching English at the University of Western Ontario in London. During that coming summer, he researched and wrote a critical study about Leonard Cohen, a writer, performer, and songwriter. "He was the most important influence on (me) as a young writer and on (my) generation." Michael has described Cohen's writing as "refreshingly unelitist."

Michael's second book of poetry, *The Man with Seven Toes,* was published in 1969 and was later performed with three speakers in Vancouver and then in Stratford. Another performance was arranged in Toronto and directed by Paul Thompson, who would work with Michael on several later projects. Michael's next volume, *The Collected Works of Billy the*

Kid: Left Handed Poems, was published in 1970 and won the Governor General's Award. In these poems, Michael merged the Western legend of Billy the Kid with his own memories of Ceylon and childhood games of cowboys and Indians. *The Collected Works of Billy the Kid* sold over 20,500 copies in Canada alone. The book was so successful that it was adapted into a play, performed first in 1974 at the Toronto Free Theater and then in 1975 at the Brooklyn Academy of Music in New York.

In 1971, just two days before he received the Governor General's Award for *The Collected Works of Billy the Kid,* Michael was fired from his teaching position at London's University of Western Ontario. "I didn't want to do a Ph.D. and they wanted me to," Michael explained. "It's as simple as that." It wasn't long before Michael accepted an assistant professorship at Glendon College in Toronto.

At this point, Michael turned to filmmaking, producing *Carry On Crime and Punishment* in 1972 and then *Sons of Captain Poetry* in 1970. After these efforts, he returned to his poetry, finishing *Rat Jelly,* which was published in 1973. "I always loved movies," Michael stated before *The Clinton Special* appeared in 1972. "It's the main source of the mythologies we have."

While working on his film projects, Michael had also started to refocus his attention on his next book project, *Coming Through Slaughter,* which was published in 1976. Stumbling upon a newspaper clipping about a New Orleans jazz musician, cornetist Buddy Bolden, Michael became obsessed with finding out Bolden's story, and in 1973 he went to Louisiana to do research on Bolden's life. The sparseness of available information fueled Michael's imagination. "The landscape of the book is a totally mental landscape," he said. "It really was a landscape of names and rumors. Somebody tells you a rumor and that becomes a truth." Clearly, Michael identified with the jazz musician. "When Bolden went mad, he was the same age as I am now. The photograph moves and becomes a mirror," he said. "The problems Bolden has are the problems any artist has at some time."

In 1979, Michael returned to Sri Lanka and started writing his memoir, *Running in the Family*, a documentation of his family history. "History is not a dead thing," he stressed about his writing. "It's always alive." The book was published in 1982, as was another novel, *Tin Roof.* Michael had gone to teach at the University of Hawaii in the summer of 1979. A year later, he separated from his wife.

In 1981, he won the Canada-Australia Exchange Award and went to Australia. The poems that evolved after the difficult separation from his wife were published in *Secular Love*, which appeared in 1984. Michael then wrote the screenplay for Robert Kroetsch's novel *Badlands* in 1977.

Since then, Michael has been teaching at Glendon College. He has also worked as an editor at Coach House Press. His novel *In the Skin of a Lion* was published in 1987. His latest novel, *The English Patient*, was published in 1992 and won the Booker Prize.

An extremely gifted and prolific writer, Michael will continue to blend genres and media in order to "use everything, every kind of art form." With this energy in his work, Michael transforms personal history and makes it come alive.

Han Ung.

"LOVE IS THE UNDERLYING THING IF YOU WANT SOME-thing strongly enough," playwright and novelist Han Ung says. "If what you want to do gives you such great joy and you love it strongly enough, that love will guide you so that you end up doing what it is that you love doing." Like a giant compass, Han's love for writing pointed him in the right direction, and there was never any doubt about what he wanted to do with his life. Though he didn't have the support of his parents, who wanted Han to make more practical career choices, Han says, "There was no way that anybody was going to deter me from writing."

The second of five children, Han Ung was born on February 5, 1968, in Manila in the Philippines. His grand-parents had immigrated to the Philippines from China, and there the Ungs "led a very middle-class, sheltered life." Raised in Manila, Han went to school until age 16 when his parents moved the family to the United States. "It was primarily to get a better life," Han said, "and to get away from the Philippines. Because we were Chinese in the Philippines—Chinese Filipino—it wasn't really our home in a way. It was, but it wasn't, either."

Han and his siblings spent their first month in the United States in Illinois with an aunt who was in medical school. Han's parents scouted for a new home and work and soon moved the family to Los Angeles. His father found work as a clerk at a utilities and parts firm. His mother worked on an assembly line in a factory. In Los Angeles, Han went to Grant public school in the San Fernando Valley. It was a tough transition for him. "Puberty plus a new country—both are tough enough on their own," Han explains, "but together, it wasn't a party." It took Han a while before he made any close friends, and at home he didn't feel very much support either. "The five of us children were very distinct individuals," says Han; "it was pretty much each on his own." Besides reading, Han watched a lot of TV and became addicted to music videos.

Not too long afterward, however, Han started to make friends at school who had similar interests and temperaments. Han describes himself as having been very shy and sort of a bookworm. "I was 16 in a new country, wearing not quite the right clothes." But by then, Han already knew that he wanted to be a novelist. "When I was very young—even when I was eight or nine—I knew I was going to become a novelist and writer," Han says. "Because even then, all my hobbies revolved around reading."

In high school, Han experienced some frustration with his studies. There were no novel-writing classes offered in high school, so Han took a drama class instead. During the course, Han wrote his first monologue, then a scene, then a complete play. His writing started to grow and he was encouraged because of the positive response to his work. "People acknowledged that I had a gift," Han explains simply. "So I started writing plays."

From there, Han was accepted into a young playwright's lab at the Los Angeles Theater Center, which at that time was a very prestigious theater. Han never graduated from high school because the school authorities didn't recognize his foreign transcript and credits. The school wanted Han to repeat another year of English study. "It was ludicrous because I came to the States and more or less, the way I speak now, is the way I did then," Han states. "My vocabulary, my accent . . . I spoke better English than most people in the class! So I decided that I wasn't going to take that." At 18, Han had taken the equivalency test and headed straight for the young playwright's lab. "So I never went to college," Han says. "I did a lot of reading and writing. It was an autodidactic, self-learning process."

Playwriting exposed Han to an art form that he never expected to work in. "I've been hammering away at playwriting since I was 16 or 17," he explains. "In the course of that time, I have grown and written about 12 theater pieces. Most are full-length plays and some are performance works, by which I mean monologues that I performed by myself." While seriously pursuing his career as a playwright, Han had also started writing his first novel.

To support himself while he wrote, Han worked first in a factory that manufactured trophies and then at an L.A. theater where he did clerical work for the company. Eventually, he was able to give up temporary work when he received a commission from the Mark Taper Forum and then a two-year grant from the National Endowment for the Arts. "I don't know if I was the youngest to have ever have gotten it," Han wonders, "but I was probably one of the younger recipients. . . . The grant enabled me to concentrate on my writing."

Han's career started to take off. In 1991, he wrote his first monologue, called *Symposium in Manila*, which was performed at both the Highways performance space in Los Angeles and at the Joseph Papp Public Theater in New York. In 1992, Han returned to the Public to do another solo piece called *Cornerstone Geography*, which he performed in 1993 at both the Portland Stage Company in Maine and then at Highways. In 1993, Han collaborated with Jessica Hagedorn, author of *Dogeaters*, on a performance piece called *Airport Music* at the Los Angeles festival. He and Hagedorn "blocked ourselves in a rehearsal room," Han recalls, "she wrote a piece; I wrote a piece. We read them to each other during the course of a week, then collated and collapsed the two separate monologues into one piece." In the summer of 1994, they performed *Airport Music* again at the Public and then at the Berkeley Repertory Theater.

In the meanwhile, two plays Han had written in Los Angeles were produced at the American Repertory Theater at Harvard in Cambridge, Massachusetts, and then in London at the Almeida Theater. These two one-act plays, *In a Lonely Country* and *The Short List of Alternate Places,* are about the days and nights of an Asian male prostitute. Han was particularly interested in having an Asian character at the center of the play without creating an exclusively Asian play. "I wanted to give space to this character so that he could exist and see what that was like without creating a politically correct checklist for him with virtue, worth, obedience, filial piety, intelligence. . . . He would be the hero simply because he'd be at the center of the play," Han states. "In the past, writers have been concerned with telling people that Asians, like any other race, are worthy of respect, too. Being of a younger generation, my concerns are different. Other people have accomplished that agenda already, so it's up to me to find a new set of goals."

In 1992, Han had three productions in the San Francisco Bay Area running at the same time. One was *Bachelor Rat;* the second was *Reasons To Live.* The third was *Symposium in Manila.* "*Reasons to Live* is about an Asian male ex-convict, who having been in prison for the last 10 years for killing his mother, is released from prison," Han says. "Unfortunately,

I have a very pessimistic view of the world—that there is a cyclical nature to destiny—and his impulse to murder causes him to kill his girlfriend."

Having recently finished performing *Airport Music* in New York and in Los Angeles, Han is currently finishing his new play called *The Chang Fragments. Swoony Planet* is also in production. Han has also just finished his second novel, *Skank Rote.* His first novel, which he wrote between the ages of 18 and 23, is called *Stranded in the World.* A chapter was excerpted in *Charlie Chan Is Dead,* an anthology of Asian American writing.

Han has been deeply influenced by Maxine Hong Kingston's *China Men* and Jessica Hagedorn's *Dogeaters.* Their work made him realize that it was possible to "be a great writer and be ethnic at the same time." Han's favorite author is Flannery O'Connor. In his spare time, Han enjoys going to the movies. He also likes going to clubs or just walking through the park, and he remains a vociferous reader. He still watches a lot of music videos. "I'm jazzed by the sensibility, the quick cuts, the music underlying it, the youthful feeling of it."

Han recently moved to New York and hopes to start exploring new art forms. He thinks screenwriting is a possibility and hopes one day to direct a music video. Directing for movies is also an avenue he'd like to explore, but until his novels get published and he has a more solid body of work, he doesn't think he'll feel really free to move on.

Jessica Hagedorn.

IT WAS NO ORDINARY HOUSE. IT WAS OLD AND GRAND, the kind of house that was usually filled with the liveliness of children and pets. It contained secret nooks and crannies surrounded by lush, tropical gardens and wildflowers. This home in Manila, in the Philippines, was a place to be explored, a place that could haunt a young girl's imagination as much as the Tagalog radio melodramas, the forbidden American movies, and the classic books of Western literature that she was exposed to. This young girl would grow up to be the writer Jessica Hagedorn, whose first novel, *Dogeaters*, would be nominated for the National Book Award and would win the Before Columbus Found America Book Award.

Jessica Hagedorn was born in Manila, the Philippines, in 1949, shortly after the end of World War II. The Philippines had been colonized by the Spanish and then by the United States before the Japanese invaded in 1941. It wasn't until 1946, after the Japanese had been defeated, that the Philippines was granted complete independence by the United States. Jessica's father, Henry William Hagedorn, ran an import-export business. His Spanish-German family were entrepreneurs who had gone to the Philippines sometime during the 19th century. Jessica's mother, Bessie Ibanez McCall, was also of mixed origin. Bessie's father, James McCall, came from the American Midwest. One of the first American schoolteachers to come to the Philippines when the Americans took over from the Spanish at the turn of the century, he was also a writer and a political cartoonist. He taught and traveled throughout the islands building schoolhouses. Stationed at Cotabato, a Muslim region in the south, Jessica's grandfather met Tekla Ibanez, a public health nurse known locally as "a one-woman health brigade." The couple fell in love, married, and settled in that southern region. Their daughter Bessie had dreams of becoming a dancer. Ultimately, she married young and gave up that dream to take up painting.

Bessie and Henry William Hagedorn were forced to flee in 1941 when the Japanese invaded the Philippines. "They fled on the last plane leaving Manila for Hong Kong," Jessica recounted. "Oh—it was so dramatic!" In fact, Mr. Hagedorn had been working undercover for British intelligence—and his wife didn't learn about it until later.

The Hagedorns lived for several years in Hong Kong and Macao, where their two sons were born. They returned to Manila soon after the war ended, and Bessie's parents, Tekla and James McCall, joined their household. Last to join the Hagedorn family was daughter Jessica Tarahata Hagedorn, born on May 22, 1949.

Jessica grew up watching her mother's hobby for painting blossom into a passion. Bessie painted constantly. "Fortunately for me," Jessica commented, "she passed this passion for art in all its media down to me at an early age." But it was also the presence of her maternal grandfather that influenced Jessica to become a writer. He introduced her to all kinds of books, so that by the age of six, Jessica had already started to write "little novels" that were typically four pages long and self-illustrated. By the age of nine, Jessica had already explored the works of writers such as Walt Whitman, Jane Austen, and Charles Dickens. Jessica had by then decided that she was going to be a writer.

In contrast to the pleasant, carefree life at home, Jessica spent her days at a Catholic girls' school taught by "rigid and fearful" nuns. Though in some ways she feels that it was "a great education," she now questions why classes were taught in English whereas Tagalog, the main native language of the Philippines, was taught as a foreign language. "Shouldn't this have been the other way around?" she asks rhetorically. In her writing now, she recalls how history books presented her with "a lopsided history of myself, one full of lies and blank spaces, a history of omission—a colonial version of history which scorned the 'savage' ways of precolonial Filipinos."

At 14, Jessica's life in Manila abruptly ended. Bessie left the Philippines with her children for the United States. They first stayed with one of her sisters in San Diego, California, but then moved to San Francisco. This was a drastic change. Coming from Manila, where she had to be accompanied by a chaperon even when she went to church, Jessica realized a freedom she hadn't experienced before. "In spite of being female, it was perfectly all right for me to explore the city by myself. . . . What I value most in Western culture has been this profound sense of 'freedom' as a woman—a freedom of movement and choice that is essential to any human being, and certainly essential for a writer."

Perhaps the most dramatic change in Jessica's early life was the sprouting of her career as a poet. It was through a family friend that several of Jessica's poems were sent to Kenneth Rexroth, a well-established poet and translator, also known as "the champion of the beatniks." Impressed with Jessica's poetry, he invited her to a dinner party at his apartment. "From the first time I walked into his apartment, with all the cubist paintings on the walls, I knew that I wanted to live in that world," Jessica said. Rexroth presented her with a book of Spanish poems that he had translated and became something of a mentor for her. "That was a real turning point for me," Jessica noted.

Rexroth took Jessica's writing seriously. He critiqued her poems, familiarized her with the writing community in San Francisco, took her to readings by other writers, and on many occasions he brought her to bookstores for buying sprees. He also opened his private library, containing thousands of French surrealist books in their original editions. Jessica devoured those books, going straight to Rexroth's library every day after school.

Jessica gave her first public performance when she was 16. At one of Rexroth's poetry readings, Jessica recalls, "He asked me to come up onstage and read a few of my poems with the band. I hadn't expected it and I was terrified but I got into it."

Rather than attend college after she graduated from high school, Jessica decided to study theater arts at the American Conservatory Theater (ACT) in San Francisco. It was there at ACT that Jessica slowly realized that "she didn't fit the stereotype of the blonde, all-American heroine," and "wasn't interested in running around auditioning for parts as hookers. I thought, I'm never going to play the big roles; it's ridiculous. But I can write, and I can create worlds." Jessica started writing seriously again, her first poems appearing in *Four Young Women,* a collection of poetry edited by Kenneth Rexroth in 1972.

When Jessica was in her twenties, she started getting involved with a community of artists and writers of color. Together, they published an anthology entitled *Third World Women* in the early 1970s. Jessica continued to write, supporting herself by teaching writing workshops at schools, jails, hospitals, and other public spaces. "Work and life were so tied together that the fun was really in all of it," Jessica explains. "It was fun and social." Two close friends were Thulani Davis, author of *1959*, and Ntozake Shange, the performance artist and author of *for colored girls who have considered suicide when the rainbow is enuf.* "Both women have been important to my development as a writer-performer," Jessica has noted. "All three of us were interested in doing poetry in collaboration with artists working in other media—dance, music, film."

Asian American performance artists who have influenced her work include Ping Chong, creator of *Nuit Blanche,* and Winston Tong. Though her writing is nothing like Frank Chin's, she thinks that their writings carry the same kind of "anger." Overall, Jessica holds to a world vision influenced by Filipino writers such as Carlos Bulosan and by the works of Amiri Baraka, Ishmael Reed, the Last Poets, and Victor Hernandez Cruz. It is South American writers such as Gabriel García Márquez and Luisa Valenzuela who she feels most in tune with because of the lyrical qualities in their writing.

Passionate about music, Jessica had found a way to bring music and poetry together. She formed the West Coast Gangster Choir. As a singer and songwriter for this "poets' band," Jessica wrote short theatrical pieces to perform between songs. This enabled the band to "combine words with music and not have it be boring or stuffy." She succeeded in creating a kind of spectacle that combined the lyrical with the visual. "I don't blame [people who think poetry is boring]; I hated poetry in school, and I thought it was taught like some dead thing," she said during an interview. "If people don't like

Jessica Hagedorn with Han Ung, rehearsing one of Ung's performance pieces.

it, I can see why they don't." With this in mind, Jessica finished her second book of poetry, *Dangerous Music*, in 1975.

Jessica continued to write and perform with her band until 1978, when she was invited to New York to do readings with Thulani Davis and Ntozake Shange in *for colored girls who have considered suicide when the rainbow is enuf*. Joe Papp, then the director of the New York Public Theater, saw the performance and asked the cast if they would like to be in a cabaret show at the Public Theater. "I borrowed clothes and stayed and stayed," Jessica explained. "The show ran for four months and finally I went back to California, packed up my stuff, sold everything that I couldn't put in the bag, and decided to try New York."

Impressed with Jessica's work, Papp invited Jessica to produce *Mango Tango*. From that point on, Jessica pursued her work as a performance artist. *Tenement Lover*, originally a song, was an expression of Jessica's experience after her move to New York: "I felt strange; people would assume I was Puerto Rican," she explained, "which is a totally different thing."

Having established New York as her home base, Jessica met and married artist and music video producer John Woo. Their eldest daughter, Paloma, was born in 1983. Another daughter, Esther, followed eight years later. Her family gave Jessica a real life-and-death perspective on the world. "You are a lot more in touch with issues in life," she explains; "it challenges you to think: is this thing I'm doing really worthwhile? Is this what I want my children to experience? It makes you care about what's happening to the world more."

When not working on performance pieces, Jessica dedicates her time to writing. *Pet Food and Tropical Apparitions* was a collection of her poetry and prose published in 1981. Selections from *Pet Food* and *Dangerous Music* were reissued under the title *Danger and Beauty,* published in 1993.

Jessica started writing her first novel, *Dogeaters,* published in 1989, after she returned to the Philippines in 1988. Until the mid-1980s, she had gone back to Manila almost every year to visit her family. During her stays, she compiled notes "about the contradictions and elements of Philippine society." She became determined to write a book. "I got reinspired. . . . The way people talked, and the food, it was all there, even the smell. It was great."

Currently Jessica is finishing her second novel and continues her busy schedule of performances and readings. Most recently, Jessica worked with Han Ung, a playwright and novelist, on a collaborative performance piece, *Airport Music.* She has also finished a book tour to promote *Charlie Chan Is Dead: An Anthology of Contemporary Asian American Fiction,* which she edited and published in 1993. She has also written screenplays, one of which was made into *Kiss Kiss Kill Kill,* an independent feature film directed by Shu Lea Cheang. In the future, Jessica hopes to complete a cultural memoir about Filipinos in America.

It is a busy life being Jessica Hagedorn—writer, performance artist, singer, and songwriter. Yet, however involved with different media, Jessica asserts, "Writing is always my base. Above all, I am a writer first. My work in other arenas helps shape me as a fiction writer. . . . It makes what I do distinctively my own."

David Henry Hwang.

"I THINK SO MANY STRANGE AND UNBELIEVABLE THINGS go on in the world that I tend to give the unbelievable the benefit of the doubt unless evidence proves otherwise," said David Henry Hwang, winner of the Tony Award for best play for *M. Butterfly* in 1988. David has applied his philosophy to his work, writing to make the unbelievable believable, describing in *M. Butterfly* a 20-year love affair between a French diplomat and a male Chinese spy whom the Frenchman believed to have been a woman. David has also written about a character who had been abducted and released by extraterrestrial beings; Chinese railroad workers on strike in 1867; and a group of Asian American actors in whiteface who plot to disrupt the opening night of a Broadway musical because a white man, who is made up as an Asian, is playing Fu Manchu. David enjoys writing about the ironies of racial and gender stereotypes. "We make certain assumptions about people based on skin color and gender. Is this some mass delusion we're all participating in?" David asks.

The eldest and only son of Henry and Dorothy Hwang, David Hwang was born on August 11, 1957, in Los Angeles, California. His father had immigrated to the United States from Shanghai in 1948. His mother grew up in a powerful and affluent family in the Philippines, and was a classical musician and piano teacher. The Hwangs met at the University of California at a foreign students' dance on Halloween. Henry Hwang founded the Far East National Bank, the first Asian American–owned bank in the United States. He and Dorothy married and moved out to San Gabriel, where David grew up with his two sisters, Margery and Grace. Originally, David's parents had tried to settle in

David
Henry
Hwang

nearby Monterey Park, but were told flat out by the owners that they would not sell to Chinese. Determined that he and his family be assimilated, Henry had his son attend the Harvard School, an elite college preparatory academy where David excelled in debate and violin. His parents were fundamentalist Christians, and David says that family life at home was like "Jerry Falwell without TV," as well as "prayers at every meal, church on Sunday and most of Saturday, Bible study midweek." Thoroughly westernized, David commented, "I knew I was Chinese, but I thought it was a minor detail, like having red hair."

David's maternal grandmother knew the tradition of "talk story," and it was through these stories that David learned about old Chinese myths and fables, as well as the history of his own family. One time, his grandmother warned David never to walk too close to the ocean, for a past relative had been stolen away and sold into slavery. David listened to his grandmother's stories, and when he was about 12 or 13 and thought his grandmother was dying, he decided to record them. After collecting her oral history, David wrote what he refers to as a "12-year-old's equivalent of a novel." When it was finished, he distributed it to members of his family. "And that was it," David remarked. Nothing was supposed to come of it.

David graduated from high school in 1975 and enrolled at Stanford University with the intention of pursuing a career in law. He realized, however, that he was always more interested in doing something involving words. While at Stanford, David attended performances at the Magic Theater and the American Conservatory Theater in San Francisco. "I was attracted to creating a world that could appear before me," David explained about his growing interest in playwriting. "Every time I went to the bookstore and found another play by Pinter or Shepard it was a new excitement, like being in love. With this passion I manage to teach myself a lot."

It was also during David's years in college that he began to explore his Asian American identity. "There was at the time a third-world consciousness, a third-world power movement," David has explained. "Particularly among Hispanics and Asians." He started to spend time with other Asian Americans who were also examining their cultural heritage. For a while, he played with an all-Asian rock band called Bamboo. They played what David referred to as "Asian American protest music."

In the summer of 1978, David attended the first Padua Hills Playwrights Festival. Under the guidance of Sam Shepard, he began to work on a play entitled *FOB*—a term that stands for immigrants who are "fresh off the boat." Sam Shepard affected David as a playwright and as a teacher. One of the first plays that David had ever read was Sam Shepard's *Geography of a Horse Dreamer.* He had also gone to see many of Shepard's plays at the Magic Theater.

David's writing professor at Stanford, John L'Heureux, encouraged him to submit *FOB* to the National Playwrights' Conference at the Eugene O'Neill Theater Center in Waterford, Connecticut. In the spring of 1979, just as David was about to graduate from Stanford, the conference accepted *FOB* for production. The play starred John Lone, the Chinese actor who would eventually star in Bernardo Bertolucci's *The Last Emperor*. *FOB* was awarded an Obie for best new play of the 1980–81 season.

After the production of *FOB*, David returned to California where he taught creative writing at a high school. It wasn't long after that Joseph Papp, the artistic director of the New York Shakespeare Festival, came upon *FOB* and decided to mount a full-scale production of the play at the Public Theater in New York City. Papp had been looking for Asian writers because of protests over the lack of Asian and Asian American material at the theater, and he took a strong interest in David's work. David was then only 23. "To have that confidence from a producer so that one is not working in a vacuum is a wonderful luxury for a developing writer," David has commented. "I think one of the most frightening things— and I've seen this in some of my friends who are writers—is going through that period when you feel you're writing just for yourself, that there's no other audience."

David starting taking courses in playwriting at the Yale School of Drama. "I felt I didn't actually have a good grounding in theater history," David has said. "It's really important to know what's come before . . . and to see what other people have done. It opens up so many more possibilities, things one may not have thought possible in the theater." David continually argues that the best education for a playwright is to see and read as many plays as possible.

In 1980, David was commissioned by the Henry Street Settlement to write a play for their coming ethnic heritage series. David wrote *The Dance and the Railroad*, which focused on a famous strike by Chinese railroad workers in

1867 in the western United States. The play was favorably reviewed and was then transferred to the Public Theater.

Family Devotions, David's third play to be performed at the Public Theater, opened on October 18, 1981. A satire about a Chinese American Christian fundamentalist family, it received mixed reviews. *Sound and Beauty* was produced in October 1983 and was greeted with praise, but did not receive the same recognition as his first two works.

The stress of having produced four plays in three years and being thrust into the celebrity limelight made it difficult for David to continue writing. "My artistic motor had run out," David said. It was also difficult to accept how he had suddenly come to be regarded as an Asian American spokes-person. "On the one hand, it was flattering . . . [but] it was no longer that I was a playwright," David explained. "I was an Asian American playwright, and my Asian Americanness became the quality [that] defined me to the public."

It was time for a break. David traveled through Asia, Europe, and Canada. While in Canada, he started work on *Rich Relations.* He also met the Chinese Canadian artist Ophelia Chong, then still a student. They married in 1985. *Rich Relations* was similar to *Family Devotions* in that it dealt with families struggling with wealth and materialism. The differ-ence was that *Rich Relations* was about a white American family rather than a Chinese American family. On the whole, the reviews weren't favorable. David took another break from theater and wrote screenplays for movies and television.

Though *Rich Relations* was David's first failure, it was also a liberating experience. "I realized, it's okay. I'm still alive. It's not the end of the world." During David's break from theater, a friend had relayed to him the true story of a 20-year love affair between a French diplomat and a male Chinese spy whom the diplomat believed to have been a woman opera singer. To David, it seemed a parody of the opera *Madame Butterfly,* and he called the play he wrote about this relationship *M. Butterfly.* David dedicated the play to his wife, Ophelia, but it was during the production of *M. Butterfly* that the marriage broke up and the couple divorced.

M. Butterfly won the 1988 Tony Award as best play of the year, as well as other awards. It earned over $35 million in the United States alone, and was one of the most successful nonmusical plays in Broadway history. Following its production, David worked on a collaborative piece with composer Philip Glass and Jerome Sirlin, a stage designer, to produce the "science fiction music drama" *1000 Airplanes on the Roof.* Later in 1988, Hwang was commissioned by the Metropolitan Opera to write a libretto for Philip Glass's new opera *The Voyage.*

As for the play that followed, *Face Value,* David commented, "Following up on success can be intimidating." Success made it possible for David to be bolder as a playwright, allowing him to show the "courage to keep trying to explore more of my own beliefs." *Face Value,* a farce about sex and shifting racial identities, was inspired by the controversy over the Broadway musical *Miss Saigon,* in which the lead role of an Asian pimp was given to a white actor who had his eyes taped back during each performance.

Disappointingly, however, *Face Value* did not open on Broadway as planned. But, perhaps because of David's chain of successes and occasional failures, he remains convinced that risks are worth taking, because he has made the unbelievable believable as he had always hoped he'd do.

David Henry Hwang

Willyce Kim.

Willyce Kim

COURAGE IS AN APPROPRIATE WORD TO DESCRIBE THE poet and novelist Willyce Kim. In her writing, she has explored all kinds of women's issues in various situations—a young child who feels dissatisfied with her role as a girl; self-discovery and love with another woman; the waste of life by diseases such as breast cancer; the forgotten victims of a serial killer. Writing has been a way for Willyce to remember and question.

The eldest of three children, Willyce Kim was born on February 18, 1946, in Honolulu, Hawaii. Her father, William Kim, was a sportswriter for the *New Honolulu Advertiser.* Her mother, Alice Lee, worked in a bank and then later for the Federal Reserve. Willyce's grandparents from both sides of her family left Korea seeking better employment opportunities in Hawaii working in the sugarcane fields. Willyce's maternal grandmother was a picture bride, chosen from a photograph by Mr. Lee to be his wife. She left Korea for a new home in Hawaii with a husband she had not met yet.

Willyce describes her early years in Hawaii as idyllic. At home, her father encouraged her to read a lot. Willyce picked up anything from biographies of sports heroes to adventure stories like *Robinson Crusoe.* She would read the legends of King Arthur and imagine herself as one of his knights. Or she would read *Tarzan,* and her imagination would leap into the wilderness of exotic jungles.

Today, when Willyce looks back, she describes herself as having been a tomboy. Beyond her backyard was a large park where Willyce could almost always be found when not at home or in school. Influenced by her father's focus on sports like basketball, baseball, and football, Willyce wasn't the least bit intimidated in joining the neighborhood boys in their afternoon games. In the park, there was also a stream where she went fishing. And for fun, after the giant park lawns were cut, Willyce and her friends would build grass huts to hang out in. At night, this club of neighborhood kids went to the movies. Willyce's favorite movie was *The Babe Ruth Story*, starring William Bendix. "After the part where Ruth died, I just cried and cried."

Nothing, however, could compare to her passion for Elvis Presley. Willyce attended his concert when his tour took him to Honolulu. She watched as he sang and realized that it wasn't even so much the lyrics that were so special, but the way he moved when he sang them. So cool. "He was the first guy to really 'rock and roll' on stage!" Willyce explains. "I was crazy about him!"

When Willyce was seven her father made a career change. Wanting to be a lawyer, he decided to attend school in San Francisco, California. The Kim family moved to San Francisco, where Willyce described the transition as "okay" because she made friends quite easily and had an aunt in the city who would take her fishing at the pier. Because there was no longer a park in her backyard, and because the weather wasn't as mild and warm as it was in Hawaii, Willyce spent more time indoors picking up new hobbies. One was collecting minerals. Willyce had always loved reading, but she now started to write as well. She managed to win a weekly writing contest for kids sponsored by the *San Francisco Examiner*. "I could probably do this," she said, after reading several stories written by kids her age. The award was five dollars. Her story was about a boy named Tommy who became a hero in a basketball game. Willyce, at the age of nine, realized for the first time that writing was really fun.

Willyce attended St. Bridget's elementary school until the age of 10, when she switched to Convent of the Sacred Heart. She remembers several aspects of her Catholic schooling, one of which was the scratchy polyester uniforms. Though uncomfortable, at least "you didn't have to stress out about what to wear all the time!" In class, Willyce found the science and math classes difficult and gravitated toward reading and English courses. Today she still wonders: "Why do we take algebra courses, anyway? I still haven't figured out a place for it in my life!" Because Willyce tended to fall behind in her math curriculum, her parents made her attend summer school to prepare for each coming year. Giving up her summers for school made Willyce hate the math courses even more.

After Willyce's father finished law school, the Kims returned to Honolulu to be near the rest of their family and to start Mr. Kim's law practice. Willyce was 13. Moving back to Hawaii was tough. She felt that she was leaving a lot behind in San Francisco. Her former friends in Hawaii were going to new schools and everyone had changed, including Willyce. She no longer had close friends as she did in California, and she made up her mind that she didn't want any, either, because she'd rather read and be by herself than be with a lot of people. It was a time for introspection, a time that Willyce refers to as her "loner" stage.

Throughout high school, Willyce also found it increasingly difficult to deal with her family. "I wasn't close to my family" Willyce explains, "and I didn't have a best friend." Her parents saw her at home alone reading all the time and they asked: "Why don't you join an after-school activity or a club through the church?" And because Willyce started to hang out with people who they referred to as "troublemakers," Willyce felt even more misunderstood and isolated. "Just leave me alone," Willyce wanted to say. She would grab a book, jump in her car, and head for the beach. "In Hawaii, the beach is the thing to do," Willyce explains. "During the summers, I'd be there from nine in the morning until six at night. . . . I lived there."

Dating was never really an issue for Willyce. Meeting boys just didn't matter that much. It was more important for her to figure out what she was supposed to be doing with her life. She'd always felt that she'd become a writer, but somehow it didn't seem a real choice. And though she was in a beautiful place like Hawaii, she was plagued by the sense that she should be somewhere else. "In California, I could get into my car and just drive somewhere," Willyce remembers thinking. "But in Hawaii, I was confined to the island." From a large and domineering Korean family, she felt as if there were only so many places she could go to get some privacy and have enough room to grow. "I felt like I was living under a microscope," she recalls.

College changed all that. Willyce attended San Francisco College for Women (now called Lone Mountain College) in 1964, majoring in English literature. She graduated with a bachelor of arts degree in 1968, and she soon made many changes in her life. "I stopped going to church," Willyce says, "because I asked myself: was it my idea, or was it my parents'?" Another question that she had to deal with was her sexuality. "Am I heterosexual, or am I gay?" Willyce soon realized that she wasn't heterosexual; she was a lesbian. "Actually, I knew all along," Willyce explained. "When I was 16, I went to a drugstore to run an errand. While I was there, I found a pulp novel with two women on the cover. It was like *Forbidden Love,* so I bought it and read it. And liked it. I thought to myself: 'Wow, I have these feelings!' " Also, every once in a while, Willyce found that she got crushes on female teachers in school.

College life in the 1960s was a time of experimentation for young people. "It was a time of free love, of questioning authority and burning bras," Willyce said. "The movement played a large part in my development and growth as an individual." She met her first woman lover, and began to apply herself to her writing and poetry. She read constantly as well. Her favorite writers included Dylan Thomas, Allen Ginsberg, Lawrence Ferlinghetti, Richard Brautigan, and Diane DiPrima. Willyce spent her free time at poetry readings, coffeehouses, and going to movies.

After Willyce graduated from college in 1968, she worked in the financial district of San Francisco as a Medicare correspondent until she started teaching in a Catholic elementary school for seven-year-olds to eleven-year-olds. She then explored other avenues of self-employment, working as a photographer making negatives for a printing company, and becoming involved in housepainting and landscaping, all the while continuing to write poetry. Willyce eventually settled into a job at the University of California at Berkeley as the stacks manager for the Graduate Library. She loves her work and has been there for 11 years. At home, Willyce lives with her longtime partner, Campbell Crabtree.

Her first book of poetry, *Curtains of Light*, was written with her sister, Carmel, and was self-published in 1971. Willyce's next book of poetry, *Eating Artichokes*, was published by the Oakland Women's Press Collective in 1972. *Under the Rolling Sky* followed in 1976. Willyce says, "Poetry's really emotional. I write about things that touch me, much of which evolved into political poems." Many of her poems deal with issues about being a woman. For instance, in *Eating Artichokes*, Willyce wrote a poem for Angela, a student she'd taught in class who was only seven but who had become dissatisfied with growing up a girl. "Angela recognized that boys get better treatment than girls—that they get better toys." Willyce recalls, "Angela asked me, 'Why can't girls wear pants all the time?'" The poem focuses on a girl who is seven but disappointed about her gender role.

Another poem, "Mount Tamalpais," focuses on the murders that were committed by a serial killer who killed 10 women over the course of more than a year. Many of those women, killed on Mount Tamalpais, had been hiking alone. "The poem was for the victims," Willyce says. "Whenever I see that mountain, I want it to always move me so that I will always remember those women who died. Died."

Another issue that Willyce writes about is breast cancer. Having suffered from the loss of two close friends who died in their early thirties and forties from the disease, Willyce says, "Wake up! Breast cancer kills a lot of women."

After writing several books of poetry, Willyce turned to prose fiction. *Dancer Dawkins and the California Kid* was published in 1985, and *Dead Heat* followed in 1988. Now, when working on a book, Willyce keeps to a very rigid schedule of writing before and after work and on weekends, always writing from seven until midnight, and sometimes even later. But in her free time, she lets her hobbies take over. "I go to Reno—I love gambling!" she admits, laughing. "And, oh yes, I love going to the racetrack!" Surprises like this are what Willyce is all about. She's filled with adventure, and it's this gusto that keeps her speaking out about issues that are important to her. Poems such as "Mount Tamalpais" reach beyond politics and into the realm of the personal.

Marie Lee

"I BEGAN WRITING ABOUT FINDING MYSELF, TO FIND OUT what I had ignored for so long," Marie Lee has said. Author of *Finding My Voice, If It Hadn't Been for Yoon Jun, Saying Goodbye,* and numerous articles and essays that have appeared in the *New York Times, YM,* and *Seventeen,* Marie has shared with her readers some of her own experiences—both good and bad— and in so doing has found a unique voice. Writing has given Marie a chance to speak out and transform some of the painful experiences from her past. Much of this has to do with coming face-to-face with her Korean American identity, an issue she began to examine once she started writing her first book, *Finding My Voice.* "If you grow up in this country as a person of color," she said during an interview, "you can't help but look at things through a prism of race."

Marie Lee was born on April 25, 1964, in Hibbing, Minnesota. She was the third of four children. During the Korean War, her father, William Lee, had served as a translator for the U.S. Army while also attending medical school. Self-taught in English, he had a dream to go to America. *Mi Guk,* the Korean word for America, literally means "beautiful country." "I think the word embodies how my father felt," Marie Lee explained. "He felt that if he went to this other country, maybe things would be better for his children. It isn't because he didn't like Korea, but that there was more opportunity." Dr. Lee's dream was realized in 1953 after he met Grace Lee at a Bible studies class. She had been in college during the war, studying pharmacy at Ewha Women's University. They married and moved to the United States, first settling in California.

The Lees were actually a very special case because the anti-Asian immigration laws were still in effect at that time.

It was through friends that Dr. Lee had made during his work as a translator for the U.S. Army that arrangements were made for the Lees to come on a student visa. At first, Dr. Lee studied in a seminary, though he was under constantly increasing pressure from the Immigration and Naturalization Service. The Lees sought a lawyer who, in the end, did nothing to help their situation. For a period, the Lees lived with the constant threat that they would be deported. Finally, however, another friend from the army who had been studying at the University of Minnesota stumbled upon news that a small, nearby mining town called Hibbing was looking for an anesthesiologist. With a population of only 18,000, Hibbing struck Dr. Lee as a nice town to raise children in. "We ended up there," Marie Lee said, explaining how they became the only Korean family in the town.

Moving to Hibbing became the first step in the Lees' efforts to become naturalized citizens. Though Asians couldn't become citizens at the time, they were able to obtain resident alien status. It wasn't until sometime after 1965 that the Lees became naturalized. Their local congressman circulated a petition throughout the town and brought it before Congress, where he pleaded that Dr. Lee and his wife, Grace, be allowed to stay in Hibbing on the grounds that Lee was "essential for civil defense" purposes.

Soon after the Lees' arrival, their first son was born. Mrs. Lee stayed at home to raise her four children, but as they grew older and went off to college, she decided that she would finish her education. Though she hadn't been able to speak English when she first arrived in the United States, she had been quick to learn, speaking only English at home with her children. She went to summer school to finally complete her undergraduate degree. Then, against her husband's protests, she went to the University of Minnesota to get her master's in adult education. For Mr. Lee, it was difficult to watch his wife assume such a nontraditional role for a Korean woman. Able to overcome her husband's more traditional bent, she is now executive director of the Minnesota Korean Social Services Agency and considers herself to be a career woman.

The mom Marie knew growing up, however, was a mom who funneled her energy into her children, her husband, and her household. Marie grew up loving basic American foods like pizza and macaroni and cheese and hanging out with her friends. Marie had, in fact, grown into the image of the all-American girl. Captain of the cheerleading team, she had a wide range of friends, and on one occasion even entered the Miss Teen USA pageant as the Hibbing representative. "The cheerleading and beauty pageant are similar," Marie explained. "I consider myself a feminist and my friends make fun of me now when they find out that I was a cheerleader. But, if taken in context of being in high school, it makes perfect sense . . . the whole thing about being a cheerleader is that you have this uniform; everyone knows who you are; and you definitely fit in."

Marie considers her high school years as some of the best times in her life. "Though I felt a great deal of pressure from my parents to do well in school, it was a time when I first felt really intense about things. . . . I could look at the sunset and feel profound about it." It was also a time for making close friends. On one occasion, she and a friend who hated their piano teacher decided they should egg the teacher's

car. At a supermarket, they talked a busboy into giving them several rotten eggs. "When we drove past the car, Patty threw all the eggs out the window," Marie recalled. "But she didn't realize that I hadn't opened the window yet!" Of course, the two of them spent the entire night cleaning up the mess in the car. Years later, at the same friend's wedding, she joked with Marie: "Remember the egg time?"

There were experiences, however, that weren't the least bit pleasant. In gym class, there had been a group of girls who made up a dance they called "Ching Chong Chinaman." They made sure to perform the routine in front of Marie and the rest of the gym class. "It was a horrible situation because I was completely passive in these kinds of situations," Marie explains. "Unlike Ellen [the protagonist from *Finding My*

Voice], who finally gets to beat up her tormentor, I sat around and took it all." On one particular occasion, however, Marie had a bunch of friends who spoke out on her behalf. "These girlfriends were really tough and smoked and they kept saying to me, 'What's your problem? Why don't you just tell them off?' " Finally, after she continued to ignore the racist slurs, Marie's friends went over to "speak" to two of the girls. "We're really sorry. Really sorry we did this," they quickly told Marie. The two girls never bothered Marie again.

Marie and her teen friends were avid readers of *Seventeen* magazine. They paid particular attention to all the makeup tips. "They tell you exactly what to do," Marie said with a chuckle. "The thing that year was that girls wore blue eye shadow and really pale lipstick. So we all did things like that. I always noticed that my friends looked fine but I looked kind of weird." Once, at a state hockey tournament, *Seventeen* sponsored a makeover for Marie because she was the cheerleading captain. Marie was excited, but found after they were finished that they had made her look really "Chinky" with lots of eyeliner extended at the corners. They also cut her hair, drying out her natural curls to pull it straight. "It was one of the first times that I realized this was the way people must see me," Marie recalled, "whereas I don't see myself this way."

Eventually, it was through *Seventeen* magazine that Marie published her first article, at the age of 16. The first story that she sold, however, at the age of nine, was to her parents, who paid her a quarter for it. Her brother had been given a new electric typewriter, and Marie received the manual hand-me-down. "The words looked so cool on paper . . . so professional," Marie remembered. "At that point, I just knew

93

I wanted to be a writer." She wrote her first novel when she was in the sixth grade, having a friend illustrate it. Marie could always think of stories and loved writing them down. Her initial reaction after *Seventeen* bought her article was that "being a writer is easy." But Marie soon found that the lucky moment was in some ways a bit misleading. "I thought I'd just send in more stuff," Marie explained. "And of course, all of it was rejected for the next 10 years." After Marie had finished her second book—with her first still unsold—she began to wonder if "maybe I wasn't meant to be a writer. Maybe writing's not that easy."

But Marie hung in there. During the period between the *Seventeen* magazine article and *Finding My Voice*, Marie graduated from Hibbing High School and went on to Smith College in 1982. From there, she transferred to Brown University, graduating in 1986.

After college, Marie moved to New York, where she worked for an economics data–forecasting company before switching to Goldman Sachs as an equity researcher. "The jobs were so I could make money and make my parents happy," Marie said. But she also felt that it takes more to be a writer than sitting down and saying, "I want to be a writer." "I felt I needed to get out and work and experience life," she now says, "because I believe you have to pay some dues."

In fact, while working full-time, Marie was also busy completing *Finding My Voice.* Waking early, she would write before work. Then after work and on weekends she would write more. She was careful to put money aside from each paycheck, planning for the day that she would eventually write full-time. This routine took a toll on Marie and she suc-

Marie's memoir, Finding My Voice, *was published in 1992. She is now working on a sequel.*

cumbed to mononucleosis in 1987. Returning home to Minnesota to recuperate for a month, Marie then returned to New York more determined than ever to finish her book. In 1991, two years after she started working at Goldman Sachs, Marie made the final decision to quit her job, establishing her career as a full-time writer.

By 1989, Marie had her book written, polished, rewritten, and ready to be sent out. But the rejection letters came back one after another. There were as many as 15 rejections and a growing, invisible cloud of self-doubt. "If you only knew what she's gone through," Mary Kim, a longtime friend has said. "She's a very private person who doesn't complain, but she's the hardest worker I know."

Author Judy Blume provided encouragement, inspiration, and advice after Marie wrote her a letter, and they continued to correspond by mail. "Keep writing," Blume wrote in one of those letters. "Don't give up . . . . It takes time and perseverance, and writing is hard, lonely work." Determined to hold onto her dream, Marie turned on her computer and began writing her second book, *If It Hadn't Been for Yoon Jun.*

Finally, Marie's perseverance paid off. Through an instructor at a writer's workshop, she was put in contact with book agent Wendy Schmaltz, who succeeded in getting *Finding My Voice* published in 1992. *If It Hadn't Been for Yoon Jun* was being published in 1993. Since then, Marie has been busy at work writing her third book, *Saying Goodbye,* a sequel to *Finding My Voice.* Marie considers *Saying Goodbye* as her "bridge" book, her step up to maturity as a writer. "As I'm getting older," she explains, "my voice is, too."

These days, in her incredibly hectic schedule of readings, school visits, lectures, mentoring other young writers, as well as involvement with organizations such as the Asian American Writers' Workshop and the U.S.–Korea Society, Marie manages to make time for weekly lessons of tae kwon do, a Korean martial art form, and Korean language classes.

In the summer of 1993, she traveled to Korea with her parents and her longtime boyfriend Karl Jacoby. On her second trip to Korea, Marie stayed for three months. She came to better appreciate and understand Korean culture and traditions—even food like kimchi, chili-peppered cabbage!

Back in New York again, Marie has started several writing projects. One book she is currently working on is written from a boy's perspective. She also hopes to write more critical nonfiction in the future. "The time period my parents lived in is very interesting and I feel compelled to try and preserve this history," she said. "People of our generation don't really know how it was to live here as Asian American people—especially through the yellow peril years during the war."

"Finding my voice" is perhaps the best description for Marie's writing in general. "The whole idea of adolescence is self-actualization and self-realization," Lee has said. "My search for identity has been a process that began in adolescence and will probably continue for the rest of my life."

Bharati Mukherjee in New York City in 1989.

WRITING OUT OF HER PERSONAL OBSESSIONS, BHARATI Mukherjee validates and acknowledges the existence of the third-world immigrant experience in America. Originally from Calcutta, India, Bharati spent several years in Canada before immigrating to the United States, where she finally established her citizenship as an American. Though Bharati has been writing since 1972, her work didn't explode onto the scene until 1988, when she won the National Book Critics Circle Award for *The Middleman and Other Stories*. This confirms a truth that Bharati has firmly held to: "Concentrate on putting out a good word. A good word will not die. Someday it will find an audience."

Bharati Mukherjee was born on July 27, 1940, in Calcutta, India. She was one of three daughters born to Sudhir Lal Mukherjee and her mother, Bina Barrerjee. The family was of the Brahman caste, the highest of five castes in Indian society. Mr. Mukherjee was a well-established research chemist and owner of a prosperous pharmaceutical company, and Bharati grew up with the social and religious privileges of wealth and caste. Bina Mukherjee, as Bharati has described her mother, was a strong and determined individual, and though "the term feminist seems inappropriate . . . [she] was one."

Until Bharati was about eight, she lived in a household shared by over 30 relatives. "Your primary identity was community identity, and you were trained to think of privacy as selfishness," Bharati has explained. "Closing the door or wanting space for yourself was considered a selfish act." The private world that Bharati turned to was in books, reading works by authors such as Leo Tolstoy, Fyodor Dostoyevsky, and Maxim Gorky.

In 1948, Mr. and Mrs. Mukherjee moved to England with their three daughters. Without the constant bombardment of cousins, aunts, and uncles, Bharati suddenly found the privacy and freedom that allowed her to pursue her literary interests. By the time she turned eight, she had written her first "novel" about a child detective. In 1951, however, the Mukherjees moved back to Calcutta. But now Bharati's mother, Bina, insisted upon moving into a home separated from her extended family. Many Indian families traditionally live within one household, consisting of extended groups of aunts, uncles, and cousins. Coming from a woman, such a notion was unheard-of and considered inappropriate. Bharati explained how this resulted in punitive "physical and verbal abuse." Apparently, however, the trade-off was well worth it; Bina Mukherjee remained insistent that her husband and children live in their own household.

Attending private schools, Bharati was introduced to writers such as Jane Austen and E. M. Forster. Nurtured by her love of literature and her parents' support, she was determined to become a writer. She entered the University of Calcutta, graduating in 1959 with a bachelor of arts degree. In 1961, she obtained two master's degrees in both English and ancient Indian culture at the University of Baroda. In an interview given in 1988, Bharati recalled an evening during the period when she was still in graduate school, when her father had invited several American scholars to dinner. "I want this daughter to be a writer," Mr. Mukherjee said, addressing a drama professor. "Where do I send her?"

It was then that Bharati first heard about the Writers' Workshop at the University of Iowa, one of the best-known writing programs in the United States. In 1961, she received a scholarship to this creative writing workshop, and there she developed her technique, style, and voice as a "third-world woman writer." While enrolled at Iowa, Bharati met a fellow student, Clark Blaise, whom she would later marry in 1963. Apparently, however, during this period at graduate school, her father wrote to tell her that he had found the perfect future husband for her. Arranged marriages were customary in Indian society. The Indian man Bharati was supposed to marry was a nuclear physicist with the "right" background. Also Bengali, he was highly educated and of Brahman caste. "If I had married this man—who is now very important in the Indian nuclear industry—I would have been a very different kind of person and a different kind of writer," Bharati has said. "If I stayed in India, I would have written elegant, ironic, wise stories which would be marked by detachment."

Bharati, however, took her life into her own hands and changed her fate. "I never could have stayed in India," she explained. "I knew from the moment I got here that I wanted to stay. I preferred unpredictability to a privileged but predictable life." Thus, on September 19, 1963, after a two-week courtship, Bharati and Clark Blaise were married. It seems that in many ways the couple was meant to be. "We have a special kind of literary marriage," Bharati explains. "There's not a moment when we're not talking literature. If I'd married a nuclear physicist, in some way I'd be a lonelier person." It was this "sameness of focus" that helped the two survive the extraordinary cultural and religious differences."

Bharati received her M.F.A. degree in late 1963. With her husband, she moved to Canada. Bart Anand, Bharati's first son, was born in 1964 and Bernard Sudhir, her second son, was born in 1967. In Canada, Bharati encountered a great deal of anti-Asian prejudice, a backlash caused by the influx of South Asian immigrants. "Indo-Canadian citizens like myself were called names, spat on, pushed or shoved in subways, and even thrown onto the tracks." After writing about racial discrimination in an essay published in 1981 entitled "An Invisible Woman," she received bags of hate mail. "Change your unpronounceable name," one letter suggested. "If you didn't play in the snow as a child you have no right to regard yourself as a Canadian," another said.

Bharati's financial situation had also caused her considerable anxiety. "For more than 20 years Clark and I have held three and four jobs per year in order to make ends meet," Bharati has commented, talking about the three teaching positions she held during the 1960s at Marquette University, the University of Wisconsin, and McGill University in Montreal, Canada. It wasn't until 1969 that Bharati obtained a position as an assistant professor at McGill, at about the same time as she obtained her doctorate from the University of Iowa. She continued to teach at McGill, steadily working her way to a full professorship in 1978. There were many difficult moments, however, such as the time when Bharati "had to calculate whether [she] had enough money to buy orange juice as well as milk for breakfast." She even considered taking a job as a chambermaid. "But then I remembered I didn't know how to drive, and couldn't get to a motel!"

Despite the demands of mothering two young boys while working for her Ph.D. and starting a teaching career, Bharati never lost sight of her dream to write. "The momentum of a work-in-progress has always carried me," she explained. "There's not a single moment when I'm not thinking stories in my head. Sometimes endings will come to me in

dreams." Drawing on her personal experiences as an immigrant woman caught between two extremely different cultures,
in 1972 Bharati published her first book, *The Tiger's Daughter*,
in which she sees her character "like a bridge, poised between
two worlds."

Other writers offered her support and encouragement.
Bernard Malamud, a longtime friend and mentor of her
husband's who taught at Harvard, was "a second father to
Clark, and he became a second father to me, too," Bharati has
said. Margaret Atwood, a well-established Canadian writer,
also played a crucial role by introducing Bharati to agent
Elaine Markson, who would eventually get Bharati's work to
the "right" editors.

Bharati's second novel, *Wife*, published in 1975, focused mainly on issues surrounding the narrator's exploration
of feminism and her struggle as a new immigrant. Bharati's
third work of fiction, however, wasn't to be written for the
next 10 years. "I didn't have the strength to say," Bharati
explained, "I'm going to do what I want to do, just write my
fiction." It was during this period that Bharati focused her
energies mainly on nonfiction essays and other scholarly
works.

After a series of near-tragic accidents, coupled with
the pressure of racial tensions against Indo-Asians, Bharati
and Clark left for Calcutta, India, to rest and recuperate.
During their yearlong stay, the couple collaborated on what
would become *Days and Nights in Calcutta*, which was eventually
published in 1977 after they returned to Canada. In the book,
Bharati points out that, "To be a third-world woman writer
in North America is to confine oneself to a narrow, airless,
tightly roofed arena."

In 1980, after determining that the situation in Canada would continue to worsen against South Asian immigrants, Bharati moved with her family to the United States, settling in Saratoga Springs, New York, where she took a position as a visiting professor at Skidmore College. From there, she went on to teach at Emory University, Montclair State College, City University of New York, and Columbia University. All the while, because she had to go where teaching jobs led her, she lived apart from her family. Her husband would soon establish his teaching and writing career in Iowa, where he lived with their two boys. Though it was difficult living apart from her family, Bharati had no other regrets about moving to the United States. It had removed that oppressive sense of fear and the "duty" to be a voice against anti-Asian violence and prejudice. She felt free to become a more multidimensional writer. This sense of freedom is evident in her third book, *Darkness*, a collection of short stories.

The Middleman and Other Stories was published in 1988, and this collection won Bharati the 1988 National Book Critics Circle Award for best fiction. Bharati became an American citizen in 1989, making her the first naturalized American citizen to win this prestigious award. Her novel *Jasmine*, also published in 1989, was inspired by the heroine of one of the short stories in *The Middleman*.

Bharati currently teaches at the University of California at Berkeley. Her most recent work of fiction was *The Holder of the World*, a novel published in 1993. The idea came to her in 1989 at a pre-auction viewing at Sotheby's antique auction house. After coming across a 17th-century Indian miniature of a blonde Caucasian woman in an ornate Mogul court dress holding a lotus blossom, Bharati found herself wondering,

"Who is this very confident-looking 17th-century woman, who sailed in some clumsy wooden boat across dangerous seas and then stayed there?" She researched this artifact, obsessed with a question that dominates much of her work: How does the immigrant, transplanted into a totally different culture, survive?

The struggle for cultural survival is the key to understanding the characters that Bharati writes about. "Mine is a clear-eyed but definite love of America. I'm aware of the brutalities, the violences here, but in the long run my characters are survivors. . . . By American, I mean an intensity of spirit and a quality of desire. I feel American in a very fundamental way, whether Americans see me that way or not."

Dwight Okita.

A SUCCESSFUL POET, PLAYWRIGHT, AND MUSICIAN, Dwight Okita describes himself growing up a "tough kid." In elementary school, he discovered a self-empowering way to overcome racist slurs. In high school, he came out to his parents and friends about being gay. Always interested in the arts, Dwight withstood years of insecurity before developing a strong sense of his own accomplishments. "People should know that many of us writers go through times when we're not strong, either. So it's a tremendous feeling to be who I am today, doing what I want to do," Dwight explains. "Being a writer or artist is a process you have to work at and define."

Born on August 26, 1958, Dwight Okita thinks it's ironic that, had it not been for World War II and the internment camps, his parents, Fred Yoshio Okita and Patsy Takeyo Arase, would never have met. Fred Okita was second generation, a Nisei, from Seattle. Patsy, also Nisei, was a native of Fresno, California. They were interned at different camps early in the war, but both relocated with their families to Chicago in search of new homes sometime after 1942. Fred Okita spent only a brief period in the camps because he had volunteered for the all–Japanese American 442nd Regimental Combat Team, one of the most highly decorated American battalions of the Second World War. After making fresh starts in Chicago, Fred and Patsy met at a Japanese American church picnic. They married and moved to Hyde Park, a city near the University of Chicago, where Fred Okita majored in anthropology. Ultimately, he pursued a teaching career. Patsy Okita started working in a bank as an accountant and later in a number of retail businesses. The couple had two sons, Clyde and Dwight.

Dwight was five when the Okitas moved to the predominately Jewish neighborhood of Hyde Park on the southeast side of Chicago. During the 1960s, Hyde Park was the site of a series of vicious killings by a man named Richard Speck. He killed eight nurses, three of whom were Filipina. Dwight was in the second grade when this happened. Television news reports said that Richard Speck could have stopped at any house. For Dwight, who lived only a block away from where the murders occurred, this was terrifying. Were there other Richard Specks out there who killed Asian Americans like him? "When you're not used to seeing many Asian Americans at all in the media, and then suddenly you see so many of their faces on TV," Dwight explained, "it's like 'Oh, God!' In my childhood memory, I thought the victims were mostly Asian American." Now a poet and playwright, Dwight has taken this experience and written it into a short play entitled *Richard Speck*.

Dwight had already started to write short poems when he was in the second grade. His first was a rhyming poem about a penny-candy store. Dwight would hang out with his best friend Keith, who was African American, and they would load up with candy from the penny-candy store near school and spend time in the playground talking. The friends were inseparable. "I remember telling my mother: 'Keith and I are one,'" Dwight said laughing, "and when she looked at me uneasily, I said, 'Oh, Mom, I'm not gay!'" Eight years later, after Dwight's family had moved away from Hyde Park and the two friends had fallen out of touch, they happened to meet on the street. "We found out that we were both gay, which we had no idea about when we were younger," Dwight recalled, "and I remember I'd felt really connected and maybe it was because we were both gay and we didn't know it!" These memories make Dwight laugh now.

Later, one particular incident clarified for Dwight that he was gay. He had watched a talk show on TV with a gay man surrounded by a bunch of religious people who told him he had to change. All Dwight could think of when watching this was, "I know how that gay man feels. There's nothing wrong with what he feels." And eventually, Dwight came to understand for himself, "That's who I am."

The family moved to Midlothian when Dwight was in the sixth grade because of the good school system there. Dwight enjoyed going to his new school, Central Park Elementary, but "we later found out that Midlothian at one time had the largest branch in Illinois of the Ku Klux Klan. And even though that organization was not active anymore, the residual prejudice was very clearly present in a lot of the kids that I came in contact with. I'd walk down the street and I'd get called 'Chink' even though I wasn't Chinese, or they'd talk pidgin English or pull their eyes back." This kind of prejudice really disturbed Dwight because he knew that those kids didn't really know better and that it was their parents' influence that caused them to act in such ways. Dwight also knew that they were young enough to learn differently and avoid prejudiced ways.

It occurred to Dwight that he could ignore racial incidents that occurred to him as if they didn't bother him, but if he didn't say something, maybe those kids would think it was because Dwight couldn't speak English. He also thought about cussing them out and learning to live with their hatred. In the end, however, Dwight set himself a challenge by doing something not only different, but self-empowering. His plan was first to make sure that the person saying the slurs realized that Dwight could speak English. Second, Dwight wanted to bring out something they had in common, something that they could both relate to. His goal was to part having laughed about something together. "Instead of avoiding kids that might be problematic and crossing to the other side of the street, I started seeking them out. It was a very different feeling—I wanted to do my experiment and I wanted to see if it would work." The opportunity finally came about one day as Dwight walked down the street and was called a racial slur. "I stopped, looked at the boy, smiled, and said, 'Hi, how are you?'" The boy, who was a bit younger than Dwight, was surprised. "Do you go to Central Park?" Dwight asked, starting a conversation. The boy said yes. "That's where I went," Dwight responded, mentioning a teacher he had the previous year whom the boy knew as well. They parted as Dwight had hoped, both laughing, and as they headed their separate ways, Dwight thought about his victory. When the boy suddenly shouted, "Hey!" Dwight thought he had declared victory too soon. "Here it comes," he thought, turning to confront the boy. The boy waved. And then he said, "Bye."

This exchange was a profound moment for Dwight. His experiment had succeeded, and Dwight knew the boy would from that moment on see him very differently. And he also knew that, whether it was devising ways to overcome his shyness, or to come out to his parents or friends about being gay, experiments were risks worth taking. He had told his parents about being gay by drawing a picture when he was 16. He wrote "gay love," "gay pride," and "gay is good" among an array of shooting stars and pointed arrows. When his mother saw it, she thought Dwight was showing political sympathy for gay people. "Oh, no," Dwight corrected, "I am gay." When Dwight confronted his father, his father surprised Dwight. He said affirmatively, "You're my son."

By high school, Dwight had developed several passions. His first was poetry, which he had turned to in elementary school because the writing of longer compositions was especially difficult for him. "It was a fluke," Dwight said. "I was bad at writing stories that made any sense, so I'd get very bad grades on my compositions. On a whim, I started writing poems at the bottom of my compositions, and my teacher started grading both my stories and my poems. And I'd get terrible grades on the stories and terrific grades on the poems, so it was more out of a grade-point consideration that I actually started writing." Dwight had also struggled with reading stories for the same reason that he couldn't write them: he got bored really fast and had a short attention span. The first book that he read from cover to cover was a collection of ghost stories. "I wasn't an avid reader," Dwight explained. "It wasn't until high school that I started to love reading." But this didn't affect Dwight's gift for possessing an impressively large vocabulary. His friends at school called him Words.

Dwight had two other passions besides writing. "I called myself a prisoner of WAM," Dwight explained. "Writing. Acting. Music." Being somewhat shy in high school, Dwight would lock himself away on weekends with his piano. Elton John was his idol and Dwight wanted to be like him. He thought: "I've got to create an album."

Dwight graduated from high school in 1976 and then attended the University of Illinois at Chicago. It was at college that Dwight pursued his third passion, acting, and majored in theater. He took his junior year off to study at different theaters, one of which was at Steppenwolf Theater Company under the direction of John Malkovich. "It was before Malkovich became a star," Dwight recalled. "I became so aware that there were really gifted actors for whom acting was effortless and that I should leave the acting to them." It was a pivotal moment for Dwight. He had already been accepted into a highly competitive acting program at New York University, but he decided to turn back to his first love—writing. Dwight graduated from the University of Illinois at Chicago in 1983 with a bachelor of arts degree in creative writing.

Dwight has written several plays. *The Rainy Season* was produced in February 1993 by the Zebra Crossing Theater. *The Salad Bowl Dance* was commissioned and produced by the Chicago Historical Society in May 1993. *Richard Speck* was produced in 1991 as a part of the American Blues Theater's anthology show *Monsters. Dream/Fast* was produced as part of the Igloo Theater's New Works series in 1987. *Letters I Never Wrote* has not yet been produced. Recently, the HBO cable network has been looking at several of Dwight's plays for their New Writers' Project.

Crossing with the Light, Dwight's first book of poetry, was published in 1992 and was nominated as the best Asian American literature book of 1993 by the Association for

Asian American Studies. Dwight received an Illinois Council Fellowship in 1988 and was also a panelist at the Asian American Renaissance Conference in 1992.

There are many artists who have influenced Dwight's writing. One of the first poets he gravitated toward in high school was Philip Levine. Later, Dwight got turned onto playwrights John Guare, Philip Gotanda, and Tony Kushner, the author of *Angels in America*. He also feels a bond with playwright David Henry Hwang, whom Dwight interviewed when *M. Butterfly* opened in Chicago. Dwight gave Hwang one of his own plays, *The Rainy Season*, which Hwang read and liked. They kept in touch and corresponded by phone and mail. "David has influenced me by being someone who has risen as a theater professional to win the Tony Award and be on Broadway," Dwight explained. "It is his visibility as someone who has broken through, and also, how he encouraged me—that he would take the time to drop notes or call me sometimes. It was very encouraging."

Though Dwight remains committed to writing for the theater, he also hopes to move in the direction of screenwriting. And though he has no immediate plans to start a second book of poetry, he says that "poetry infuses everything I write." "I'm happy to see myself moving every day, as a writer, closer and closer to where I want to be," Dwight says. "I've always had a lot of luck with my writing career. . . . It seems that it has all come full circle."

Laurence Yep.

Laurence Yep

"I DID NOT ORIGINALLY PLAN TO BECOME A CHILDREN'S writer about Chinese Americans," Laurence Yep has explained. "Instead, I began as a science fiction writer because, as a child, I found that only science fiction . . . dealt with strategies of adaptation and survival—strategies I had to practice each time I got on and off the bus." Laurence describes these science fiction stories as unconscious attempts to search for his identity as a Chinese American. The focus, as with many of his later stories, is on the alienated, the outsider.

Yep was born on June 14, 1948, in San Francisco, California. His father, Yep Gim Lew, or Thomas, which was his Anglicized name, immigrated from Guangdong Province, China, when he was ten. Laurence's paternal grandfather had already been in California for a few years and had become partners with an Irishman in a pharmacy. Laurence's mother, Franche Lee, was born in Lima, Ohio, and was raised in Clarksburg, West Virginia. Her family had originally come from Nanping Province, China, in search of better opportunities. The Lees ran a family laundry before moving to California. Thomas Yep and Franche Lee met and became friends at Galileo High School. Thomas went on to attend junior college for a year, but because of the harsh realities of the Great Depression, he left and started working as a playground director in San Francisco's Chinatown. The Lees married and had their first son in 1939. After saving and borrowing money from friends and family, the Yeps opened their own corner grocery store. Laurence was born with daily chores already waiting for him.

"My chief job was feeding the beast," Laurence said, referring to stocking the store shelves. There were other places he would rather have been, and other things he would rather have been doing. There were times he worked begrudgingly, wishing that he could be riding around in Jezebel, the family's '39 Chevy, which could deliver him to Golden Gate Park where there were a petting zoo, slides, jungle gyms, pony rides, and a merry-go-round. Laurence would stock shelves and remember his last visit to his favorite place, Ocean Beach. "My mother would roll my pants up my legs and tell me I could only go out to the point where the pants started to get wet," Laurence related in his autobiography, *The Lost Garden*. "Of course, when she wasn't looking, I would roll the cuffs up even higher until not only my pants but my shirt was soaked."

The family store meant constant chores and a lot of hard work. And though Laurence hated it then, he realized many years later that it did a great deal for him. When he became a writer, he found that having a daily routine was something he was already accustomed to. Writing was a habit, just as work in the store was. And sometimes writing wasn't fun. "Writing a novel is a hard process—like a long-distance runner running a marathon. I know I can't reach the finish line that day," Laurence explained. "Instead, I have to be patient, trying to complete a shorter stretch of writing."

The Yeps lived in a largely black neighborhood, but Laurence commuted by public bus to a bilingual Catholic school in Chinatown. There, Chinese was taught in school, and when Laurence was put in the beginner class, he resented it so much that he swore to himself to get good grades without learning or remembering anything. At home, his parents spoke English and he thought of himself as "American," but when he watched TV he would see cartoons of Chinese laundrymen with exaggerated, slanted eyes wearing black pajamas. These daily shifts from one world to another, and the conflicts they produced, made life really difficult. He became a Catholic, and later an altar boy, in the hope of attaining some kind of guidance and resolve. In *The Lost Garden*, Laurence's memoir, he tells of a time when his brother purchased a Chinese puzzle for a friend. It was in the shape of a box, and before giving it, Laurence's brother used the instructions to take it apart and then reassemble it, leaving the instructions tucked inside afterward. Laurence explains how "the more time I spent going back and forth between my own neighborhood and school, the more I felt as if I was like that box with the necessary instructions locked up inside me and no way to get at them."

Laurence had always loved reading. His parents read to him, but for every story they read, he had to read one back to them. Also, because Laurence was asthmatic, his mother would read to him each time he had a bad attack. It was in this way that Laurence was first introduced to *Pirates in Oz* by Ruth Plumly Thompson. The fantastic story saved him. "The asthma was so severe that I was convinced I was going to die; but as I slipped into a half-sleep, I fell into a strange logic of dreams and reasoned that I could not die because my story had not yet come to an end." These stories inspired Laurence. "They dealt with the real mysteries of life," he said, "like finding yourself and your place in the world."

From that point on, Laurence leaped into a world of science fiction. He would go through libraries looking for science fiction books, reading through all of them, making his way through both the children's and young adult collections.

Robert Heinlein and Andre Norton were his favorite authors because of their funny characters and the exotic, mysterious worlds in their stories.

Laurence attended St. Ignatius High School for Boys, where he was placed in the honors class. He worked hard and good grades were important enough to his family that he was exempted from many chores at the family store. Laurence made sure to get good grades from then on to keep from returning to his previous duties. High school was also a time when Laurence started writing. His English teacher announced that in order to get an A in the class, the students would have to get a story or poem accepted by a national magazine. Though none of the students were published, Laurence was struck as if by a fever. He had always loved making up stories, so writing became a challenge. "Writing did not make a lightbulb appear over my head. It did not make me scribble away in a frenzy as if I had just been zapped by an electrical cattle prod. Nor was it a religious ecstasy. No symphony of cymbals crashed in climax when I reached the final paragraph." What happened instead was that Laurence started to write as if to solve the puzzle within him that he had never understood before. He started to see the Chinese American person that he was, a boy who grew up in a black neighborhood, who was always either too Chinese or too American to fit in anywhere.

In 1966, Laurence attended Marquette University intending to major in journalism. There, Laurence felt both homesick and isolated. "Of some twenty thousand students," he wrote, "I doubt if there were more than a hundred who were not white." He transferred to University of California at Santa Cruz, and received his bachelor of arts degree in

1970. It was during his college years that Laurence sold his first science fiction story, receiving a penny per word.

Three years later, after a stack of rejections from different editors, a close friend who worked in the junior book department at Harper & Row suggested that he write a science fiction novel for children. Laurence wrote *Sweetwater,* which became his first published book. A bit of inspiration came from having stumbled upon some information about author Mark Twain before Twain had broken into his writing career. "I was used to thinking of him as a white-haired genius," Laurence commented, "but in fact in his younger years he had failed at almost everything he had tried. . . . He contemplated suicide." Laurence stuck it out, and then after *Sweetwater* was published he decided he wanted to try something new. He had come across articles about a Chinese American aviator who built and flew his own plane in 1909. Drawing on this little bit of information, he wrote *Dragonwings,* which was published in 1975 and won the 1976 Newbery Medal. He later adapted this novel into a play which toured across the country with the Berkeley Repertory Theater.

Laurence's relationship with his friend Joanne was one that he described as similar to the situation in the movie *When Harry Met Sally.* The couple fell in love and married. In the meantime, Laurence had completed his doctorate in 1975 at the State University of New York at Buffalo, where he wrote his dissertation on the early novels of William Faulkner.

Laurence's second book of fiction, *Child of the Owl,* was published in 1977 and won the Boston Globe–Horn Book Fiction Award. Extremely gifted and prolific, he has written over 30 novels and plays, including *Sea Glass,* published in 1979; *The Green Darkness,* published in 1980; *The Dragon of the*

Lost Sea, published in 1982; *The Serpent's Children,* published in 1984; *Dragon Steel,* published in 1985; *Dragon Cauldron,* published in 1991; *Dragon War,* published in 1992; and *Dragon's Gate,* published in 1993. His adult novel, *Seademons,* was published in 1977. And undoubtedly there will be more to come.

Further Reading

Chan, Sucheng. *Asian Americans: An Interpretive History.* Boston: Twayne, 1991.

Gee, Emma, ed. *Asian Women.* Berkeley: Asian American Studies, University of California, 1971.

Golub, Caroline. *Immigrant Destinations.* Philadelphia: Temple University Press, 1977.

Kitano, Harry H. L., and Roger Daniels. *Asian Americans: Emerging Minorities.* Englewood Cliffs: Prentice Hall, 1988.

Perrin, Linda. *Coming to America: Immigrants from the Far East.* New York: Delacorte, 1980.

Reimers, David M. *The Immigrant Experience.* New York: Chelsea House, 1989.

Tachiki, Amy, ed. *Roots: An Asian American Reader.* Los Angeles: UCLA Asian American Studies Center, 1971.

Takaki, Ronald. *From Different Shores: Perspectives on Race and Ethnicity in America.* New York: Oxford University Press, 1987.

Takaki, Ronald. *Strangers from a Different Shore: A History of Asian Americans.* Boston: Little Brown, 1989.

Index

PICTURE CREDITS

RONALD TAKAKI, the son of immigrant plantation laborers from Japan, graduated from the College of Wooster, Ohio, and earned his Ph.D. in history from the University of California at Berkeley, where he has served both as the chairperson and the graduate adviser of the Ethnic Studies program. Professor Takaki has lectured widely on issues relating to ethnic studies and multiculturalism in the United States, Japan, and the former Soviet Union and has won several important awards for his teaching efforts. He is the author of six books, including the highly acclaimed *Strangers from a Different Shore: A History of Asian Americans,* and the recently published *A Different Mirror: A History of Multicultural America.*

CHRISTINA CHIU is a writer and editor who has worked for the Brooklyn Museum, the Asian American Writers' Workshop, Children's Television Workshop, and Scholastic, Inc. A graduate of Bates College in Lewiston, Maine, she currently lives in New York City.